T0063443

A *Journey towards* Greater Happiness

Other works by Venkatachala I. Sreenivas, M.D.

ON The PATH TO BECOMING A PHYSICIAN
Acute Disorders of the Abdomen
Diagnosis and Treatment

A Journey *towards* Greater Happiness

VENKATACHALA I. SREENIVAS, M.D.

PARTRIDGE

A Penguin Random House Company

Copyright © 2014 by Venkatachala I. Sreenivas, M.D.

ISBN: Hardcover   978-1-4828-3493-2
               Softcover   978-1-4828-3494-9
               eBook   978-1-4828-3492-5

All rights reserved. No part of this book may be used or reproduced by any means, graphic, electronic, or mechanical, including photocopying, recording, taping or by any information storage retrieval system without the written permission of the publisher except in the case of brief quotations embodied in critical articles and reviews.

Because of the dynamic nature of the Internet, any web addresses or links contained in this book may have changed since publication and may no longer be valid. The views expressed in this work are solely those of the author and do not necessarily reflect the views of the publisher, and the publisher hereby disclaims any responsibility for them.

To order additional copies of this book, contact
Partridge India
000 800 10062 62
orders.india@partridgepublishing.com

www.partridgepublishing.com/india

Contents

Part 1

Part 2

Part 3

To

All those who have and are contributing
for the happiness of others

Preface

Desire for happiness is universal and our quest for happiness is nothing new. Approximately 2600 years ago a prince renounced his kingdom, left his young wife and his new born son in quest of a solution for human unhappiness disenchanted with the royal pleasures at his disposal. After practicing austerities and while in deep meditation he became a Buddha, the enlightened one. Then he proclaimed to the world, "Hear ye my fellow human beings, I have great and good news for you. I have found a means for overcoming sorrow and for attaining permanent happiness." The path he showed was appealing and millions became his followers and he still has a large following. Buddha was not the only one or the first one to embark on the quest for permanent happiness. He was preceded by sages of India thousands of years earlier. They too had shown the way to permanent happiness and the path they discovered is contained in the Vedas, the earliest recorded documents in human history. The surprising question is why humanity is suffering from unhappiness even though its remedy has been available for thousands of years. The awakened one himself has answered this puzzling question. He said, "The path for permanent happiness is open to all. However the journey is strenuous. There is no magical method to make it easy. Moreover no one else can make the journey on your behalf.

You yourself have to undertake the journey." We want quick results with minimum effort on our part. We are not interested in or committed to a long strenuous journey. This is the reason why happiness has eluded us.

Just as health is our natural state so too is happiness. Disease is an intruder of health; unhappiness that of happiness. In order to eradicate a disease we have to know its causes, diagnose it by its symptoms, take preventive measures to avoid it and implement therapeutic measures to cure it. Similarly to eradicate unhappiness and enjoy happiness we should become aware of its causes. This aspect has been dealt within the first part of the book.

We are an inseparable integral part of the creation which is an organic whole like the human body. Therefore we have to function as a part of the whole and not as separate entities. However we are conducting ourselves as separate independent entities thereby infringing upon the law of creation. There is a penalty to be paid for infringing any law and in case of laws of creation the penalty is unavoidable. The penalty we pay is unhappiness. The second part of the book deals with the measures we have to take to align ourselves with the laws of creation. For aligning ourselves we need a cognitive change. The needed cognitive changes and the means for developing the cognitive changes are dealt in this section of the book.

The life history of great people serves as an inspiration and provides guidance to change ourselves for the better. It is aptly said that a picture is better than thousand words. As a source of inspiration and guidance in our quest for greater happiness the life history of three persons is presented in the third part of the book. Of these one character is mythological and the other two are historical. There are many lessons to be learnt from the study of these three characters and are highlighted in chapters 22-25.

What I have presented is what is already known but not taken advantage of. With the intention of finding ways and means for improving my own level of happiness I started my investigation. The material I have gathered has propelled me a little further towards the cherished goal. I have realized that the goal cannot be reached in a hurry. It is a slow process. It requires patience and constant alertness. The material I have gathered is presented in a book form with the hope that it may be of help to others. The sages of India dealt with the question of human happiness extensively and recorded their impressions in Sanskrit texts. I have liberally used those sources. The Sanskrit terms for many concepts have been indicated in italics. The purpose is to compensate for the difficulty in translating words from one language to the other. Furthermore, those familiar with Sanskrit terms may find it interesting.

Columbus, Ohio.

Aug 18th 2014   Venkatachala I. Sreenivas, M.D.

Acknowledgements

In preparing the book I have received help from many quarters and would like to acknowledge at least some of them. I have benefited by the teachings of their Holiness Swami Dayananda Saraswati, Swami Paramarthananda, Swami Pratyagbodhananda Saraswati, Swami Tatvavidatmananda Saraswati and Swami Viditatmananda Saraswati. I have to thank Dr. Manavasi N. Parthasarathi for his thought provoking discussions and explanation of concepts in the ancient texts in modern language. I am indebted to Sri. Sree M. Aswath for his exposition of the scriptures. My thanks to all the authors whose writings helped me in consolidating my thoughts. I am especially indebted to my wife Nagarathna; my daughter, Dr. Mytheli Sreenivas; my son-in-law, Dr. Pranav Jani; and my lovely granddaughters Meenakshi Jani and Savita Jani for their love, affection and support. My sincere thanks to the staff of Partridge Publishing India for their help and cooperation in publishing this book.

I have for the sake of convenience and consistency used masculine gender in situations applicable to both genders. No gender discrimination is intended.

Transliteration guide.

अ a   आ aa or A   इ i   ई ii or I   उ u   ऊ uu or U

ऋ R   ॠ RR   ऌ lR   ॡ lRR

ए e   ऐ ai   ओ o   औ au   अं aM   अः aH

क k   ख kh   ग g   घ gh   ङ G

च c   छ ch   ज j   झ jh   ञ J

ट T   ठ Th   ड D   ढ Dh   ण N

त t   थ th   द d   ध dh   न n

प p   फ ph   ब b   भ bh   म m

य y   र r   ल l   व v

श z or sh   ष S or shh   स s   ह h

Part 1

nahi Gnanena sadrusham

(There is nothing equal to knowledge)

We are endowed with power to know (*Gnana shakti*), power to desire *(ichA shakti)*, and the power to act (*kriyA shakti*). In order to desire an object first we should know about it. We can never desire that which we do not know. People who were living one hundred years ago could not have desired computers since they did not know anything about computers. In order to gain what we desire we should have a clear knowledge of what we want, where to find it and be capable of mobilizing the needed resources for achieving it. The more we know about these aspects of our desired object, the greater the chance of achieving it.

1

Introduction

We all want to be happy. To be happy is a natural and legitimate desire. Ancient Hindu scriptures declare that pursuit of happiness, called *kAma* in Sanskrit, is one of the desirable universal human goals. Much later Thomas Jefferson wrote "...They [people] are endowed by their creator with certain inalienable rights; that among them are life, liberty and pursuit of happiness." Now this statement is taken as a human right all over the world.

To be happy is a natural desire but what constitutes happiness varies from person to person and for the same person from time to time and under different conditions. If asked to define happiness each one of us will have our own definition. But we all have experienced happiness as well as its opposite—unhappiness—sometime or other during our lives regardless of being a man or a woman, young or old, rich or poor, scholar or a simpleton, a saint or a sinner. Indeed all our actions throughout our lives are motivated either for gaining happiness or for gaining freedom from unhappiness. For the sake of happiness some hoard money and others contribute to charity; some marry and others divorce. It is for happiness that cheaters cheat; robbers rob; drunkards drink; drug addicts resort to drugs; spiritual seekers practice austerities and the penitent repent. For ages human beings have tried and are even now trying to achieve happiness both individually and collectively through religion, politics and economic manipulations. In the pursuit of happiness, Americans spent 118 billion dollars in 2012 for foreign travel. They spend close to $ 25 billion per year to attend sporting events and purchase 140 billion dollars worth of recreational equipment. Yet the goal has remained elusive. Since 1972 only about one third of the Americans describe themselves as "very happy" according to a survey funded by the National Science Foundation. At best, we experience transient happiness but not enduring happiness. We are not satisfied with transient episodes of happiness in our lives; we want to experience enduring happiness. This desire is expressed in all fairy tales by the invariable ending sentence, "They lived happily ever after."

Despite human struggle by different means, throughout ages, enduring happiness has remained elusive. But human beings have not given up the hope of achieving enduring happiness in spite of overwhelming odds against such a possibility in our lives. That hope is kept alive by religions by the promise of a life of permanent happiness in heaven after our departure from this world. This faith, based on hope, has remained strong even in our present science oriented society —a society which demands verification for acceptance of any opinion.

Several questions are worth pondering. Why is it that we are not satisfied with transient experiences of happiness but cling to the hope of gaining enduring happiness, if not here, than in the hereafter? Why has enduring happiness remained elusive? Is it possible to achieve more sustained happiness, if not permanent happiness or is it a utopia? If it is possible, why have we not succeeded? Why some people remain happy even when their life is full of adverse circumstances and others unhappy even though blessed with a more comfortable life? Answers to these questions would empower us with a better understanding of happiness and will be of help for improving our state of happiness.

2

Why We Seek Happiness?

The universe we live in and experience is very vast. Compared to the enormity of the universe, we as individuals cannot but feel small and insignificant. The smallness and insignificance makes us feel that we are limited. And as limited beings we feel insecure and threatened, a state called *apurNa* in Sanskrit. We are limited in our physical strength, intellectual power, and in our resources. For example, even the rich people think that they do not have enough money and strive to make more. Furthermore we are limited in space. What it means is that when we are in America we cannot be in Africa or any other place at the same time. We are limited in time also. There was a time when we did not exist and there will be a time when we cease to exist. And how long we exist is uncertain and is not in our control. All objects in addition to space and time limitations are limited by their own nature (*desha, kAla, and vastu paricheda*). A rose has rosiness. A rose cannot be a carnation or a carnation a rose. We are no exception. We are limited by what constitutes humanness. As humans we can neither be angels nor brutes. In addition as humans we are limited by our gender, age, physical features, and intellectual capacities just to mention a few. We experience the universe as well as our limitations. We are not content and comfortable with our limitations as it makes us feel insecure. The insecurity causes fear. We desire security. Desire to be secure gets translated into action. All our actions are to overcome our limitations. In our attempt to overcome limitations of our knowledge we have built educational institutions. Any activity which increases our knowledge is dear to us. That is why gossip is very popular as it provides juicy knowledge about others! To overcome our physical limitations we have designed and built tools. For example, to overcome the limitations of our eyesight we have built telescopes and microscopes; flying machines and ships to overcome our limitations in flying and swimming respectively. We are spending enormous amount of money and effort in medical research to overcome our time limited life span and live a little longer.

All our actions are prompted by our desire to overcome our insecurity and limitations. When there is an obstruction for the fulfillment of a desire we become angry. When the desire is fulfilled we become greedy. We want to preserve what we have gained; gain more and we are reluctant to share our gain with others. We compare our loss with the gain of others which gives rise to jealousy. While gain can make us arrogant loss can generate hatred towards others. In summary, from insecurity come all our psychological problems such as desire, anger, greed, jealousy, hatred, etc. We cannot live happily with all these psychological problems.

Every object in the creation has qualities which may be inherent or incidental to it. For instance water when it comes in contact with fire becomes hot. Heat of water is an incidental quality. Water starts loosing heat as soon as the contact with fire ceases. However water never loses its inherent quality of wetness. In nature no inherent quality is a burden. All objects remain at ease and stable with their inherent qualities but not with their incidental qualities. There is a tendency to retain inherent qualities and give up incidental qualities. The corollary is that anything we want to give up must be a burden to be unloaded and is not our inherent nature. For example a disease is a burden but not health. We want to get rid of disease which is incidental to our nature and maintain health which is our original inherent nature. Therefore anything we are comfortable with is our inherent nature. We are comfortable being happy and uncomfortable being unhappy. Therefore happiness must be our inherent nature. It is natural to be comfortable with our inherent nature and therefore we seek happiness.

If happiness is our inherent nature, logically we should be happy always. But our experience is that we experience happiness only occasionally by coming in contact with objects of the world (by the word objects, people, and experiences are also included). Regardless of how tragic anyone's life may be, no one is denied moments of happiness. By analyzing the dynamics of happiness we gain knowledge of happiness. Knowledge is power. The power we gain by the analysis of the dynamics of happiness can be harnessed to achieve and maintain happiness and avoid unhappiness. For gaining knowledge of anything we should have a clear understanding of what we are looking for and where to look for it. Happiness is no exception. Therefore, let us commence analyzing as to what is happiness and where to find it.

3

The Source of Happiness

It is our experience that when we were young we became happy when we got a candy, a balloon or a toy etc. As we grew older the objects that made us happy changed over the years. And these objects included a bicycle, driver's license, admission to prestigious educational institutions, a well paying job, agreeable spouse, home, name and fame just to mention a few. It did not escape our notice that objects and people made us happy and based on this experience we have been conditioned to look for happiness in the outside world of objects, people and experiences. Our conclusion is that happiness is in the world outside of us. However this conclusion needs closer scrutiny.

There is no object in the world which can be called happiness. If there was such an object every one of us will be going after that object to be happy. Furthermore, there is no object which can be considered a source of happiness. An object which may be a source of happiness for one may be a source of unhappiness for someone else. For example for someone who likes apples it will be a source of happiness but for someone who dislikes apples it will be a source of unhappiness. In other words the same object will be a source of happiness for some and a source of unhappiness for someone else. Nor is happiness an attribute of an object as blue color is an attribute of the sky. If happiness was an attribute of an object that object should invariably provide happiness to all in all places and at all times and under all circumstances just as sugar tastes sweet to all, at all times and at all places and under all circumstances. Furthermore, happiness is not confined to a particular location or place. A particular place may be a source of happiness to some but a source of unhappiness to others. I know of a couple whose adult daughter had passed away causing them great grief. They had lived in a house for many years with their daughter. She had grown up in that house. There were many fond memories of their daughter associated with that house. The husband wanted to sell the house and move away from the house as it brought memories of his departed daughter and made him sad. He wanted to move away to forget the memories and start his life afresh. The memories haunted him and the house had become a source of unhappiness for him. In contrast, the wife cherished those memories and did not want to part with them. For her the house and the memories associated with it was a source of happiness. She was as adamant to stay in that house as her husband was to move away from it. The house was a source of happiness to the wife and a source of unhappiness to the husband.

Nor is a particular time a source of happiness despite advertisement of "Happy hour" by pubs. For a person on vacation at a seaside resort early morning may be a happy time especially if he is looking forward to enjoy a beautiful sun rise. He will gladly get up early to watch it. However the same early morning hour will make him unhappy when he has to get up early to go to work especially if he wanted to sleep a little longer.

It must now be clear from the above observations that neither a place, nor a time or an object in the external world we experience is endowed with happiness as an attribute. The whole external world is nothing but a combination of time, space, and objects. But we do experience happiness by our contact with the external world. The question then is how to explain this paradox.

Everything in the creation can be grouped into two categories—"I" and "other than I". "I" is the experiencer and the "other than I" is either experienced or which can be experienced. "I" the experiencer, am one and the objects I experience are many and varied. From the previous discussion it is clear that no object in the creation has happiness as its attribute and no object can make everyone happy all the time under all circumstances. But "I" experience happiness or unhappiness by coming in contact with some objects under certain conditions. **So by the process of exclusion I, the experiencer, must be the source of happiness.**

If I am the source of happiness where is it located in me? Is it in any organ or is it a product of an organ such as bile is the product of liver? No biochemist has isolated happiness as a product of any of our organs. No radiologist who sees through a living body with his X-ray machines has visualized happiness during the course of his examinations. No one who has dissected human body has found happiness in the dissected specimen. In order to know the location of happiness within us requires a different type of dissection— dissection not by knife of steel but by knife of knowledge and discrimination.

It is important to recognize that the experiencer "I" is not a single entity but a composite entity with four personalities each with its own distinctive values and demands. In the ascending order of their subtlety they are: physical personality, emotional personality, intellectual personality, and spiritual personality. Although they are separate personalities, at the time of an experience they work so quickly and simultaneously making their recognition as separate entities difficult. Let us consider the example of an experience of being rudely offered a delicious candy to understand these four personalities. Under such circumstances the physical personality may like to taste and eat the candy and enjoy it. But the emotional personality will resent the rudeness with which it was offered and refuse to eat it. Intellectual personality remembering the warning that sugar is bad for health may want to avoid eating it. Spiritual personality may caution that succumbing to temptations of sense objects is a hindrance for our spiritual growth and the temptation should be resisted. What may bring satisfaction to one personality may cause dissatisfaction to one or more of the other personalities causing stress and strain. The subtler the personality level the deeper and greater the satisfaction. Therefore the demands of the grosser personality are sacrificed for those of the subtler personalities.

The words pleasure, joy, happiness and bliss although often used interchangeably have their own connotation. Pleasure is dependent on our five senses. As an example, pleasure is the sense of good feeling we experience by eating delicious food; by being near a fire place on a cold wintery night; by being in an air conditioned room on a hot day; sleeping undisturbed on a comfortable bed; or taking a leisurely ride on the county side on a bright autumn day. In short it is enjoyment through our senses and dependent on objects, people and circumstances. Happiness derived from sense pleasure and enjoyed by the physical personality is the grossest. It is highly developed in animals. No man can ever eat with the same gusto as that of a wolf or a dog.

Joy is very similar to pleasure but has its origin in our mind (emotions) and intellect. We experience joy when we or our near and dear ones are recognized for some achievement. We experience joy when we find answers to problems be they mundane like solving a crossword puzzle or as profound as making a scientific discovery. As we evolve and become refined our ability to enjoy sense pleasures gets diminished. As we evolve the goal becomes love and reason involving the emotional and intellectual personalities. When one is identified with the emotional personality mind expands to include or accommodate the welfare of others. The feeling of love and kinship for others provides satisfaction subtler than what is gained by physical indulgence. In proportion as the higher faculties develop the power of enjoying sense pleasure becomes diminished. Our lower impulses and tendencies get sublimated. A mother donates her kidney despite the physical pain and discomfort it causes her, to her child in need of a transplant out of love and for the emotional satisfaction of seeing the child alive. When identified with intellectual personality we develop discrimination. Emotions and physical pleasures are governed by discrimination taking into consideration their effect on oneself and on the society.

More subtle than emotional pleasure is the intellectual pleasure. Nathan Hale, an American revolutionary in the war for independence, was caught and hanged by the British. His last famous words before being hanged were, "I only regret that I have but one life to give for my country." His regret was not that he was losing his life but he had no more than one life to give to his country. Nathan Hale is only one example among many who for the sake of their intellectual conviction have sacrificed physical comforts of their home, emotional security of their relations, their very precious lives and ascended to the gallows with a smile on their face. Similarly there are instances of scientists fired up with an idea having sacrificed their physical and emotional comforts while engrossed in the pursuit of their intellectual quest.

Based on the degree of self centeredness we can group people into five categories as mineral, vegetable, animal, human and divine people. Mineral man is gross, lethargic and consumed in sense gratification at the cost of his kith and kin. Vegetable man is also selfish but cares for the wellbeing of his immediate family. Animal man's identification includes not only his family but also his community. He means well to all those who come within his fold. He is an angel for those who are within his boundaries but a devil to those outside his boundaries of identification. Human man embraces within his hold much larger segment of the population like a nation. Such men are responsible for wars since they do not identify with the entire humanity. Spiritual men are rare. They have no trace of selfishness. They embrace all regardless of caste, color, or nationality. Their compassion extends to all creatures under the sun. Such men have merged their individuality with the unifying existence of the whole.

The happiness we gain at physical, emotional and intellectual level depends on external factors and shares certain common characteristics. Because of the shared common characteristics they are grouped as *preyas* in contrast to the happiness enjoyed at the spiritual level. The happiness enjoyed at the spiritual level is called *sreyas* and differs from that of *preyas*.

Happiness derived from external factors *(preyas)* has certain drawbacks. They are:

1. Mixed with unhappiness *(Dhukha mishritvam)*: Whatever happiness is gained from external factors, it is mixed with sorrow. To gain

the object of happiness is a struggle; preservation of what has been gained is a struggle. Furthermore the thought of losing the gained object can be a source of worry robbing our peace of mind and happiness. We can never be sure of possessing the desired object forever. Either we are separated from them from their loss or by our own death since we are mortal.

2. Not satisfying (*atruptikaratvam*): No matter what we have gained does not completely and permanently satisfy us. It may cause boredom after sometime by law of diminishing return. For example the first candy we will eat with relish. The second candy will not have the same appeal as the first one and after a few candies we become nauseated and do not even want to look at them. What we may have gained leads to comparison and we will find that someone else has more than we what have. Such a comparison leads to unhappiness. Our ability to desire is limitless but our ability to fulfill them is greatly limited leaving us dissatisfied and unhappy. Another feature is that of gradation of happiness which is another source of unhappiness. For instance imagine someone who is looking for a piece of furniture. That person will not be happy until it is found. When the furniture is found the person will be happy (*priya*) but will be unhappy that the furniture is not in his possession. When the furniture is possessed the person becomes happier (*moda*) but still there will be unhappiness since it is not where the person wants it to be. When the furniture is brought home and while enjoying the furniture the person will be happiest (*pramoda*). But by law of diminishing return the happiness gets diminished over a period of time.

3. Dependency (*bandhakatvam*): Dependence on external factors for
    our happiness converts them from luxuries to necessities. In the
    absence of the object we depend upon for our happiness, we feel a
    void and feel unhappy. The greater the dependency the lesser our
    independence. It is like getting addicted. When the first cigarette
    was offered to us we had the power to say no to it. We were the
    masters. But once we get addicted to smoking we lose the power to
    say no to a cigarette. Once addicted, cigarette will have power over
    us. From being masters we will have become slaves. To be happy,
    what we need is freedom and not dependence. Even animals want to
    be free. They do not want to be tied down. A Sanskrit wise saying
    (*subhashitam*) states:

    sarvam paravasham Dhukham sarvam Atmavasham sukham
    etad vidyAt samAsena lakshanam sukha dhukhayoho.

What it means is that dependence on external factors is a source of
unhappiness since the external factors may not satisfy our needs or may
not be available to us and finally enslave us. Self dependency is the sure
source of happiness. Therefore to be happy we should become independent
of our dependence on external factors. We can never become completely
free from our dependence on others for our physical needs. However we
can and must free ourselves from our psychological dependence on others
for our happiness.

Mahatma Gandhi used to keep a set of six towels and no more for his
personal use. After being imprisoned for several years he returned to his
ashram. Those who were looking after his ashram during his imprisonment
had kept eight towels for his use. Immediately he asked them to remove

the extra two towels. He is an example for us to emulate a man who was happy by decreasing his necessities. Happiness does not lie in multiplying our necessities but in keeping them to a minimum. Each one of us has to decide between what is necessary and what is superfluous; useful and wasteful; beautiful and vulgar. It cannot be imposed on us by others. If we are totally in the struggle for subsistence or if we are totally absorbed in the struggle for accumulation then our capacity to happily participate in life gets diminished.

Yayati was a noble and learned king of ancient times. He was happily married to Devayani, the daughter of sage Shukracharya. Devayani had a friend named Sharmista. In course of time Yayati and Sharmista fell in love and they wedded in secret. When Devayani came to know of Yayati's wedding with Sharmista she felt betrayed and went back to her father, Shukracharya. Angered by Yayati's behavior Shukracharya cursed him to become an old man and lose his youth. Yayati was deeply saddened and begged Shukracharya to take back the curse. The curse once uttered could not be taken back but Shukracharya made a concession. The concession was that Yayati could exchange his old age for the youth of someone willing to do so. Puru, one of Yayati's sons, agreed for the exchange and Yayati enjoyed sense pleasures for many years. Then Yayati realized the limitations of sense pleasures. He gave back his youth to his son Puru saying, "Dear son, sense pleasure is never quenched by indulgence any more than fire is extinguished by pouring oil on it. For peace and happiness one should certainly renounce craving and seek that which neither grows old nor ceases even when the body ages." Yayati illustrates the limitation of *preyas* and his yearning for *Sreyas* based on his experience in life.

It is not my intention to belittle the importance of *preyas* in our lives but only to draw attention to its limitations. No doubt we derive some happiness by coming in contact with objects of the world. The happiness so derived is comparable to the happiness a frog enjoys in the shade under the open hood of a cobra. The happiness so derived has limitations. We can be separated from whatever we consider as a source of happiness by any number of causes including our inevitable and inescapable death. With death hovering over us and ready to snatch us at any moment without any notice leaves us with a sense of restlessness and unhappiness at a constant subliminal level. We rationalize that feeling of unhappiness at subliminal level as normal since we practically find everyone around us in the same situation. Yayati recognized the problem concerning *preyas* when he said, "For peace and happiness one should certainly renounce craving and seek that which neither grows old nor ceases even when the body ages." Recognition of a problem is a prerequisite for its solution.

The subtlest aspect of our personality is spiritual. Happiness at the spiritual level ceases to be transient and is enduring. It is called bliss. Attainment of such a state is called state of *purNatvam*. At this level there will be full integration of our different personalities. Spirituality is the life center around which all activities of the body, mind, and intellect revolve. **Therefore to attain the highest degree and duration of happiness we should aim at developing our spiritual personality.**

Alexander had heard a great deal about the wonderful sages of India who were men of self realization. A self realized person is the one who has attained the zenith of spirituality. When Alexander had conquered parts of India he was keen on meeting one such sage. After some searching, Alexander was led to such a person living all by himself with no possessions of his own. Alexander was thrilled at the sight of the sage. He asked the sage to accompany him to Greece. He lured the sage with wealth, comforts, pleasures and anything the sage wanted. The sage with a smile on his face said to Alexander, "Oh king, I lack nothing. I give joy to the world and not the other way round." Alexander was confused and when he failed to convince the sage to move to Greece he was enraged. He threw the sage in prison. Alexander was warned by his counselors the dangerous consequences of his sacrilegious act. Heeding to the advice of his counselors Alexander went personally to the prison to meet the sage. There he found the sage as happy as he had found him before imprisoning him cheerfully basking in sunlight falling into the prison. Alexander apologized and requested the sage to forgive him. He was truly repentant. He said to the sage, "Oh sage, I have wronged you. Please allow me the privilege of satisfying at least one of your wishes. Then my conscience will be appeased." The sage was moved at Alexander's sincerity and his true repentance. And on his repeated insistence the sage said, "If you want to do something for me please move a little bit and let the sunlight fall on me."

The sage described epitomizes the highest level of happiness one can achieve. The sage was satisfied in himself and with himself as the source of happiness and had become a fulfilled person (*purNa*). He was not dependent on external factors for his happiness. There was nothing that anyone could take away from him to make him unhappy or give him to make him happy. Such a person will not work for happiness but work out of happiness. He had gained *sreyas* which is enduring. The sage presented here serves as an example of the ideal to be reached. However we will not reach that level instantaneously and to reach that level it takes a lot of time and effort on our part. We have to move gradually from our physical personality to spiritual personality through our emotional and intellectual personalities for gaining and enjoying enduring happiness. Any attempt on our part will propel us towards our goal of enduring happiness with incremental increase in our degree of happiness.

4

What is Happiness?

As a prelude to understanding what happiness is we should clearly understand the difference between our needs and wants. Needs are those things that are essential for our survival and growth like food, water, air etc. Wants are those things that are not essential for our survival, but are extra features that gratify our desires. For example, we need clothing to protect us from the elements. Clothing is a need. And this need is satisfied by any ordinary inexpensive clothing. It does not require fancy clothing. But the desire to wear designer clothing is a want. We can never free ourselves from dependence on others for our needs but we can free ourselves from our wants. The dividing line between needs and wants is not a sharp one and each one of us has to discover it for ourselves. It cannot be imposed by others.

Suppose you are walking in a shopping mall without any intention of purchasing any particular object. Your attitude towards objects in the shopping mall will be one of indifference. However you see a shirt on display and you are attracted to it. You want to posses it. At that moment you become a seeker of that shirt. You are the seeker and the shirt is the sought after object. As a seeker you are a wanting person. So long as the division between the seeker and the sought exists, the wanting person persists. A wanting person cannot be happy until the seeker and sought division is eliminated. You buy the shirt and feel happy. At that moment the seeker and sought division is resolved. What made you happy is not the shirt but the elimination of the wanting personality in you. Let us analyze this experience of happiness in a little more detail.

When we see a table our mind will have table thought or table *vrutti*. When we perceive a table we say, "This is a table." And the sentence, "This is a table" clearly identifies the table as an object. We do not say, "I am a table." I, the subject perceiving the table, am different from the perceived object. On the contrary when we are happy we say, "I am happy" and not, "This is happiness." We reserve the term this or that to refer to objects. If happiness was an object like a table we should have said, "This is happiness" indicating that happiness is other than ourselves. But that is not the case. Happiness is not away from us and it is our very nature. But we seek objects for purpose of becoming happy conditioned that happiness is outside of us in objects. The sought after object makes us happy for a time being by fulfilling a particular desire. However soon another unfulfilled desire takes its place. Thus one desire leads to another desire. For example we see a man is driving. He is driving not for driving sake but with the desire to reach his work place in time. His desire to reach his work place in time is dependent on another desire. That desire is to please his boss by his punctuality. His desire to please his boss is dependent on the desire to retain his job. The desire to maintain his job is motivated by a desire to earn money. Desire to earn money is dependent on his desire to provide for his family etc.

Our understanding of ourselves is that we are limited and hence insecure. We try to overcome our insecurity by trying to overcome our limitations. As long as we feel limited or think we are limited we remain a wanting person, wanting to overcome our limitations. We want freedom from our limitations. Our lives are governed by our wants. What we want varies but the fact remains that we all remain as wanting persons throughout our lives. So long we remain a wanting incomplete and insecure person we will not be acceptable to ourselves. Being unacceptable to ourselves we cannot be happy. We want to be acceptable to ourselves. What this means is that to become acceptable to ourselves we have to be different than what we are. We seek to become a different person. Thus we become the seekers. So long as there is a wanting person in us division between a seeker and the sought is inevitable. When we gain a desired object we feel happy. At that moment the division between the seeker and the sought is resolved. Division ceases to be. The wanting personality has temporarily receded into the background and momentarily we are freed from our sense of limitation and insecurity. Such experiences also happen even if we have not gained anything material such as looking at a beautiful scenery or when we have helped someone in distress without ulterior motives. During such moments of happiness what we are experiencing is a pleased secure personality. The pleased secure personality is acceptable to us unlike the wanting insecure personality. In other words when we feel that everything is in harmony as it should be, that there is no need to rearrange things then we are happy. **Happiness consists not in becoming but in being.** Unfortunately this state does not last long. Soon our wanting personality makes its appearance in the form of a new desire. The new desire may be to maintain the happiness gained or the desire to share it with someone else. As soon as a new desire rises the seeker sought division reappears and we lose our happiness.

We, human beings, have a highly developed mind. It makes us conscious of ourselves. It also makes us judgmental about ourselves and others. To make a judgment one must have norms. We must have a standard. If we were given a mango to taste and if we had not tasted a mango earlier we cannot make a judgment as to whether that mango is good or bad. We lack a standard to assess the quality of the mango. But when we taste the next mango we will have a standard to compare with. Then we can say that the mango we tasted is good or bad. Since we have experienced moments of happiness those moments become our standard. We want to maintain that standard all the time. It will be akin to an athlete who has established a record and he cannot settle for anything less. He knows his potential. Similarly, once we have realized our potential for happiness we cannot settle for anything less. We cannot settle for unhappiness and the struggle to become happy continues.

Presence or absence of material objects does not bring happiness or unhappiness. The role of objects concerning our happiness was well analyzed and understood as far back as 5000 years ago. The dialogue between sage Yagnavalkya and his wife Maitreyi as recorded in Brhdarnyaka Upanishad attests to this fact. Sage Yagnavalkya was a great scholar. He had two wives named Maitreyi and Katyayani. One day he decided that it was time to dedicate himself totally to a life of meditation and contemplation to attain eternal happiness (*Moksha*), the highest goal to be achieved by man. He called his two wives and told them in affectionate terms about his decision to pursue the life of a renunciate. He further told them that he had divided his property into two equal halves and each of them will be heir to one half of the property. Then Maitreyi questioned him whether property (wealth) gives enduring happiness. To her question he replied that wealth does not give eternal happiness. Further he expounded on the topic by saying that people seek objects not for objects sake but for their own sake. What this means is that our seeking of objects and experiences is secondary and subservient to the primary goal of gaining a pleased secure personality. What we love and value most is not the objects and experiences but ourselves. We are the most beloved to ourselves. We do everything to please ourselves. Even social service which may benefit others is undertaken to please oneself. Sage Yagnavalkya makes this point by saying to Maitreyi "*patyuh kAmaya pati priya bhavati.*" Translated to English it means that the wife becomes dear to husband not for wife's sake but for husband's sake alone and vice versa. The wife remains an object of happiness so long as she is able to evoke a pleased personality in the husband. When she ceases to evoke a pleased personality in the husband she will no longer be an object of happiness. The object (wife) being the same she should have remained beloved all the time if she was loved for object's (her) sake. Love towards wife changes depending on whether she evokes a pleasing personality in the husband or not. Once this principle is understood it becomes clear why people fall in and out of love and proves that objects do not have happiness to give us. **Happiness is inside of us and not outside of us.**

All our desires are a reflection of our sense of incompleteness or limitation. Happiness can be defined as a state of enjoying a pleased secure personality, a personality free from sense of limitation. Objects and experiences merely evoke such a personality. That is their contribution. All our desires are to overcome our limitations. Once limitations are overcome there remains no desire. Such a state of desirelessness is called state of *purNatvam*. How can we achieve that state?

We try to gain a desired object under two circumstances. First, when the desired object is away from us. The second circumstance is when the object of desire is with us but we are unaware of its presence. Although the object is with us, in our understanding it is away from us and hence the search goes on. In effect it is as though the object is far away. The means required for gaining the desired object is different in the two circumstances. In the first instance action on our part is required and in the second instance only knowledge. As soon as we come to know that the desired object is with us the quest ceases; no action is needed to stop the seeking.

It has been previously made clear that happiness is not in the outside world; happiness is inside us. Indeed happiness is our nature. During moments of happiness we are established in our true nature. Happiness is only a state of a pleased mind free from sense of limitation where there is no seeking and the seeker and sought divide is no longer present.

If happiness is our true nature we need not seek it outside of us. All we need to do is claim our true nature. If we were to create sound in the form of noise or music we have to do something. But to create silence we do not have to do anything. Silence will automatically ensue as soon as we stop creating sound. Sound arises from silence, is sustained by silence, and then merges in silence. Silence is the natural state and sound is a disruption of silence. Since our nature is happiness, just as heat is of fire, there is no need for us to achieve it. It is already an achieved fact. However we are unaware of the fact and are unhappy. Therefore we feel that happiness is something to be achieved. We become seekers of happiness because there are factors obscuring the fact that our nature is happiness. For us to be happy what all is needed is to remove those factors that are obscuring our understanding of our true nature. We have to get rid of our false notions about ourselves and understand who we are.

5

Who Am I?

"Know thyself," Said Greek philosophers. "I am the knowledge of the Self among the different branches of knowledge," Declared Sri. Krishna in Bhagavad Gita (10:23) proclaiming the importance of knowing oneself. This question "who I am?" has been extensively investigated by our sages of the past. The legacy of their insight is available for us to take advantage.

If I were to ask you, "Do you know who you are?" you are likely to say, "Yes I do know who I am. As a matter of fact who else knows me better than I do?"

"Who are you then?"

"I am Rama."

"That is your name. You were not born with that name. Your parents gave that name to you. They could easily have given you any other name. You have a name for transactional purposes. Now do you have a name or are you the name? What you have is a name. I am not interested in what you have. I am interested in who you are. Please tell me who you are."

"I am the son of so and so."

"In relation to your father you are a son but in relation to your own son you are a father. Are you a father or a son? You may be related to someone as an uncle, a husband, a brother etc. I am not interested in your relationships. I want to know who you are."

"I am a doctor."

"You have a profession. You were not born as a doctor. What were you before becoming a doctor? You have acquired some skills and on the basis of those skills you are called a doctor. I am not interested in the skills you have acquired. I am interested to know who you are."

"I am the president of such and such a company."

"President is a post which is occupied by different people at different periods of time. Are you the post or are you occupying the post of the president. Who are you occupying the post?"

I can continue in this fashion with many questions. Suffice to say that every time we are asked as to who we are, we give an identity in relation to something else. In relation to our education we are doctors, lawyers, accountants etc. In relation to our fathers we are sons. In relation to our sons we are fathers. In relation to religion we are Hindus, Christians, or Jews etc. In relation to citizenship we are American, Indian, or British etc. Our identity based on relationship or association is a role we play and the roles we assume are many. It is similar to an actor assuming different roles. Behind all the changing roles there is an actor who is constant. The roles are relative and the actor is the absolute. The roles we assume based on relationships and associations are our relative identities. Behind our relative roles there is an absolute entity which does not change just like an actor behind all the roles he assumes. Who is the actor behind all the roles we happen to play? When asked as to who we are we all begin our reply "I am…" These two words are common to all of us and then we keep adding something or other which may number in the hundreds. And we have mistakenly taken for granted that the roles we play as son, father, employer etc. as "I".

Our happiness depends on our interaction with the world. And our reactions depend on how we look at ourselves as illustrated by the story of king Vikramaditya. He was known for his wisdom. Once he sought the hand of a beautiful princess. To gain her hand he had to face a challenge and the challenge was to recognize the princess among seven maidens looking exactly like the princess. He accepted the challenge. On the appointed day he was presented seven maidens all of them looking alike. Vikramaditya dropped his gold ring from his finger and six of them bent down to pick it up. The one who did not bend down to pick up the gold ring was identified as the princess. The difference in the behavior of the princess and the other maidens was determined by what they thought of themselves. Even though the six maidens were dressed like the princess they thought of themselves as servants and they acted according to what they thought of themselves to be.

The question as to who is "I" was systematically and extensively investigated by our ancient sages many thousands of years ago by different methods of analysis. Two of the methods will be presented here. One method is called *drk drushya viveka*. This method of analysis postulates that what is seen (*dryshya*) is different and distinct from the seer (*drk*). They started the enquiry by reducing the whole creation to two categories viz., "I" the subject, the seer and everything other than "I" which is the object seen. Subject is the knower and the object is the known. Anything known or knowable constitutes an object. The subject is one and the objects are many and varied. Thus sun, moon, stars, trees, flowers, etc. are all objects known to "I"— the subject. It is possible that one may raise an objection by saying that you are seeing me and I am seeing you and therefore the subjects are also many. But this objection is untenable because what we are mutually seeing is our physical bodies which are objects of our perception. By further enquiry the objective nature of our physical bodies will be established.

Is Our Physical Body a Subject or an Object?

As far as objects other than our physical bodies are concerned we are very clear in our understanding that they are different and distinct from us. Even though our child, our spouse and our possessions are very dear to us there is no doubt about them as objects distinct and different from us. We do not mistake them as "I". They are clearly objects of our knowledge. This understanding is clearly reflected in our speech by our saying "my child" "my wife" "my house" etc. and not "I child" or "I spouse" or "I house". There is no confusion about subject –object differentiation since we have no sense of "I" in them. However with our bodies we have "I" sense and this causes confusion. When an object like a table is touched we do not feel we are touched. On the contrary when our body is touched we feel we are touched. When our body is fat we feel we are fat; when tall we are tall etc. When our body moves we feel we have moved. So we take our body as "I" since there is "I sense" in our physical body. Does the body know it is tall, fat etc. or do we know the body is tall fat etc? We know the fatness of our body as well as its other attributes like color of skin, length, aches and pains. The body and its conditions are known to us. The physical body is as good an object of our knowledge as any other object. Therefore the body being known like any other object it should be different and distinct from the subject "I". So we have to conclude that we are not the body—an unnerving conclusion. However we should go to where truth leads us.

If we are not the body are we the sense organs with whose help we objectify the body? The conditions of our sense organs are also known to us. We know whether our eye sight is sharp or dull; hearing is good or bad etc. Sense organs and their condition are also objects of our knowledge and therefore different and distinct from the knower "I".

Then is the mind "I" which receives sensory input from all the sense organs with all its thoughts and emotions. But again the condition of the mind—sad, happy, angry, agitated, calm etc.—is known. The condition of the mind being known it belongs to the category of an object and therefore it is not "I". Then can we conclude that ignorance is "I"? We are ignorant of many things. Let us for example take Sanskrit language. If we do not know that language we know of our ignorance of Sanskrit language. Our lack of knowledge—ignorance—is also known to us and hence it cannot be "I".

Then who is this "I" who is aware of our physical body, sense organs, emotions, thoughts, and our ignorance? The "I" is the subject.

Let us look at this "I" from another point of view in order to gain greater clarity. We will look at this "I" from the three states of our experience—waking state (*jagrata avasta*), dream state *(swapna avasta)* and deep sleep state (*sushupti avasta*). These three states will be examined taking into consideration, in each state, the condition of the mind, nature of experience and the dominant medium of experience. Mind is divided into four parts depending on the function it is performing. When it is functioning as the receiver and coordinator of information from sense organs it is called mind (*manas*). *Manas* then presents the gathered information to intellect *(budhihi)* for taking necessary action. Once an action is taken a result follows. Ego (*ahankAra*) is the sense of doer of action (*karta*) as well as the enjoyer of results of action (*bhokta*). The whole experience is stored as memory (*chitta*) which can be recalled at a later time. The following example will make this concept easily understandable. Suppose we see a candy. The presence of a candy is reported to the mind by the eyes. *Manas* presents this to intellect *(budhih)* and the intellect is responsible in deciding as to what to do with this information. Intellect decides that the candy should be eaten. Message will be sent to organs of action to procure the candy and eat it. We will be a doer (*karta*) when procuring the candy and an enjoyer (*bhokta*) when enjoying the taste of the candy. The whole experience of seeing the candy, procuring it and eating it and enjoying its taste will be stored in memory for possible future recollection.

Waking State

In this state mind is fully functional. All the four aspects of mind will be operational. The mind, through sense organs, will be dealing with external world which is concrete and tangible. We experience the tangible objective world—a world which is available for others also to experience. In this state we enjoy both doership and enjoyership. Physical body serves as the medium of experience. In addition we will be aware of our inner world of emotions and thoughts through our mind. In this state we will be transacting both with the external and internal world.

Dream State

Dream is dependent on our experiences during waking state. It is born out of our impressions gathered during our waking state. In dream state no new experience is gained. What may appear as new is the result of permutations and combinations of what we have experienced in the waking stage. What is seen as a result of permutations and combinations is mistakenly interpreted as new knowledge. For instance we may see in dream a man with horns and interpret it as new knowledge. But we have seen men and we have seen horns. We have also seen men behaving like horned animals. In dream we rearranged them and saw a man with horns. What we might have imagined may also be visualized in the dream state. Suppose during waking state we have fantasized giving a million dollars to someone near and dear to us then we may see it happen in our dream state. The world we experience in dream is intangible and private. It is available only to the dreamer and to no one else. Dream is memory based. Therefore only memory (*chit*) aspect is functioning in this state. The other three aspects of mind are not functional.

Deep Sleep State

In this state no aspect of mind is functional. There is no experience of external world of objects or internal world of emotions. Mind remains dormant. The experience is one of blankness. That is why we can say on waking up that we slept well but not during sleep. Even though in deep sleep state the body and mind were not functioning, on waking up we will know about the condition of our sleep. So there must be some other entity in us which was aware of our sleep. This entity is the "I". The following table summarizes the salient features of the three states.

	Waking state	Dream state	Deep sleep state (dreamless sleep state)
Condition of mind.	All four aspects functioning.	Only memory aspect functional.	Mind non functional.
Nature of experience	Tangible world of external objects and intangible world of emotions and thoughts.	Intangible world based on memory.	Blankness.
Medium of experience	Physical body along with its contained sense organs and mind.	Mind (Only chit) aspect.	Neither body nor mind.

The subject "I" is that entity in us, that is aware of all the three states of our experience as well as our body, mind, and intellect (BMI) complex. The subject "I" is the knower of body, mind, intellect, and the three states of our experience. Our body undergoes change throughout our lives. The infant body we had when we were born is imperceptibly replaced successively by childhood body, youth body, adult body, and senile body. While our body changes the sense of "I ness" in the body remains throughout unchanged.

It is the same "I" inhabiting all these different bodies. The entity within us which is aware of our BMI complex, our three states of consciousness, and all the other changes going on is called the soul (*Atma* or spirit). Whatever is not soul is made up of matter and is called *anAtma* which includes among other things our BMI complex. We as individuals are indeed a combination of both soul and our BMI complex (*Atma and anAtma*) each with its own distinctive characteristics.

One of the characteristics of BMI complex (*anAtma*) is its constant tendency for change. It is unstable. The change may be fast or slow but change there will be and is unavoidable. In the span of one short day a butterfly is born, lives, and then dies. On the contrary our sun, the longest lasting object in our solar system was formed billions of years ago, will exist for several billions of years yet to come and ultimately disintegrates and dies. Our thoughts are no exception. Thoughts are objects of our knowledge and they undergo constant change. Each thought has its birth, life span, and death. It is not possible to have a single thought that will never disappear. All changes can be recognized and appreciated only in relation to something which is constant without undergoing any change. For instance when we view a movie all the changes we experience takes place on an unchanging screen. The screen does not get affected by any changes that take place in the movie. Flood seen in the movie does not wet the screen nor does fire seen in the movie burn it. It remains the same despite all the changes seen in the movie. Soul provides such an unchanging background for the BMI complex to undergo all the changes without itself undergoing any change. Another familiar example is our travelling in a car. When we are in a moving car, with reference to the car we do not seem to be moving since we and the car are moving at the same speed. Only with reference to stationary objects like trees and buildings can we appreciate our movement by our changing position in space in relation to some fixed object.

The second characteristic of BMI complex is that it lacks awareness of itself or others. It is insentient. However our BMI complex appears to be sentient. It is important to realize that the sentiency exhibited by BMI complex is borrowed from the soul which alone is sentient. We know that moon is not self luminous. However on a full moon night moon looks bright and gives out light. We call it moon light. But in truth moon light is sun light reflected by the moon and in the process moon looks as though self luminous. Such is the situation with BMI complex. When the soul departs from the body, the body becomes insentient and disintegrates.

In order to have knowledge of objects we need a means of knowledge. The sense organs serve as the means of knowledge by direct perception. We know that a book exists because we see it through the sense of sight and feel it by sense of touch. Based on our perceptions we draw inferences which further add to our knowledge. Now if I were to ask you, "Do you exist?" Your answer will be in the affirmative. How do you know you exist? Is the knowledge of your existence based on sensory perception or inference? You will know that you exist with all sense organs shut. As a matter of fact it is because of you that the sense organs are functioning. You intuitively know that you exist without the benefit of perception and inference. You do not need anyone to confirm your existence nor will you be convinced of your nonexistence if the whole world were to say so. You are aware of your existence and this sense of being is called consciousness or awareness.

Consciousness is nonmaterial in nature. Being of nonmaterial nature it is subtle. The subtle nature of a thing is determined by its pervasiveness and its resistance to destruction. Let us consider the example of water. Ice which is the solid state of water occupies a limited amount of spce and can be easily crushed by an iron hammer. Water in its liquid form is subtler and would cover a wider surface area compared to that of ice. Hammer cannot break liquid water. All it can do by striking water is to create a splash which is only a temporary disturbance in water. Water vapor, the subtlest form of water, is more pervasive and occupies a larger area. Iron hammer has no effect on it. On the contrary the water vapor by permeating the hammer can cause it to rust and destroy it.

Of all the objects we experience, space is the subtlest. It is most pervasive and not subject to destruction. Space accommodates every object. All objects ranging in size from a small atomic particle to huge galaxies spanning several thousands of light years exist in space. We can do things in space but not to space. However space does not have consciousness. It is not aware of itself or others. On the other hand we are conscious of space. In other words space is in our consciousness. Space is accommodated in our consciousness. Therefore consciousness which accommodates space must be subtler than space. It is the subtlest and cannot be destroyed.

Only matter has properties which can be perceived by our senses. Consciousness being non-material in nature does not have properties which can be perceived by our senses. Consciousness requires a medium for manifestation just like electricity needs a bulb for its manifestation. However electricity does not get destroyed by the destruction of the electric bulb. Human BMI complex provides the most advanced medium for manifestation of consciousness. Just as electricity does not get destroyed by the destruction of the bulb, consciousness too does not get destroyed by the destruction of the BMI complex it enlivens. It continues to exist even after the body is destroyed. **Non-manifestation does not mean non-existence. Soul being the subtlest is immortal.**

It has been previously pointed out that we are a combination of BMI complex and soul each with its own different unique characteristics. We have the choice of identifying with our BMI complex or with our soul. Identification with something means becoming one with it by constantly believing, thinking and then ascertaining we are that. The choice we make has tremendous implications for our happiness. We want not just transient happiness but enduring happiness. Whatever is perishable and transient like our BMI complex cannot give us permanent happiness. Therefore for enduring happiness we have to seek it in what is permanent and not in what is perishable. Unfortunately happiness eludes us because we are searching for it in a wrong place like the woman in the following parable.

Once upon a time an old lady lived in a village. Her neighbors thought that she was somewhat weird. One day she was searching for something in the street in front of her hut under the street light. Someone seeing her searching asked her what she was doing. She told, "I am searching for my lost ring." That person joined her in her search. As time passed by, several other people with the good intention of helping the old lady find her lost ring joined in the search. When they could not find the ring after searching for sometime one of them asked her as to where she had lost the ring. She replied, "In my hut".

"Then why are you searching for the ring in the street?" asked the bewildered people.

"That is because the light is better here than in my hut. I can see things better here. Therefore I decided to search here."

We may laugh at the behavior of the old woman. But we are not too different from that old woman when it comes to our own search for happiness. For any search to be successful one should know where to find what is being searched.

BMI complex is perishable and has limitations. If we were to identify with BMI complex we will suffer from all its limitations. Since BMI is limited in space, time and in attributes we will suffer from all these limitations. The limitations of BMI make us small and insecure. Since the limitations of BMI complex are not acceptable to us we try to overcome them. We seek to be different than what we think we are. Seeker sought division persists and we remain unhappy. If on the other hand if we were to identify with our soul which is not subject to decay and death, we will be freed from the limitations of BMI complex. Then we realize that the BMI complex is only an instrument for our transaction with the world. **Limitations of our instruments are not our limitations. We are much more than our instruments.**

Although the advantages of identifying ourselves with our soul are obvious and is necessary for our enduring happiness, it is not easy. Our identification with our BMI complex is very strong and deep rooted. It is very difficult to overcome this identification. Sri. Krishna points out that rare is the person who strives to identify with the soul and rarer still is the person who succeeds. The difficulty is not without reasons. Our senses which are extrovert in nature are naturally attracted to and comprehend the gross BMI complex and not the subtle soul.

When two things are intimately associated with each other it is not easy to distinguish their separate identity and recognize the superiority of the one over the other. This is the situation with soul and BMI complex. However we have to understand what our true nature is—soul or BMI complex. It has been previously pointed out that what is intrinsic is one's true nature and what is incidental is not one's true nature. Intrinsic nature is never a burden. We are most comfortable with our true nature. For example health is our intrinsic nature and it is never a burden for us. We do not try to get rid of health. We are happy when we are healthy. On the contrary disease is not our intrinsic nature. It is incidental and is a cause of our unhappiness. It is not acceptable to us. We try to get rid of disease. The material BMI complex is perishable and the nonmaterial subtle soul is imperishable. No living organism wants to die and perish. All living organisms including man wants to live at least a day longer and strives for that goal. So mortality is unacceptable for us. Hence it is an incidental nature to us. Since soul is immortal and since immortality is acceptable to us, it should be our intrinsic nature and not the BMI complex.

Our misconception concerning consciousness is a stumbling block in identifying ourselves with our soul. Only matter which is gross has properties which are perceivable by our senses. Consciousness which is subtle cannot be perceived by our senses. Consciousness is inferred by observing a conscious entity. In this respect it is akin to life. We cannot perceive life as such but we infer the presence of life by observing living beings. Since consciousness is dependent on BMI complex for its expression it is natural to mistake that consciousness is a product of BMI complex. Such a conclusion is made more plausible by our observation that mineral world lacks consciousness; it is vaguely seen in plant kingdom and is unfolded in animal kingdom reaching its peak in man. The more advanced the BMI complex the higher is the level of consciousness. However the conclusion that consciousness is a product of BMI complex is not without flaws. There are reasons to believe that consciousness is not the product of BMI complex but its producer. What has evolved is not consciousness but the medium for its manifestation. We know that sensory stimuli are converted to electrical impulses and are transmitted to the brain through nerves. However, the transition from excitation of brain cells to subjective experience remains unexplained. It is a mystery.

A mother had two sons. One was a scientist and the other a poet. In the course of time the mother died and the sons buried her. They planted a rose bush on her grave. Both of them visited their mother's grave a year later. There were many beautiful flowers in the rose bush they had planted. Seeing the flowers the scientist son said, "The chemicals in my mother's body is nourishing the flowers." But the artist son cried out, "Oh mother you have so much love in your bosom that even after death you are nourishing the flowers as you nourished us during your life." The mechanism of transmission of sensory impulses was not different between the two sons but the experience was very different. How to explain different responses to the same stimulus? The experience is very private and defies experimentation. The physical world we experience is actually nowhere but in our own consciousness in the form we experience it. It is only approximately the same world as seen by others in their consciousness. Each of us has direct experiential knowledge and from this we postulate the physical world. We explain the differences in our postulated world by ascribing it to color blindness, deafness, or hallucination etc.

In the progression of evolution transformation of one species to another is accomplished with addition of lot more information which cannot arise by itself. It is not possible for insentient matter to add information. So it must be imparted from a non-material conscious intelligent source which is something superior to BMI complex. That conscious intelligent source is soul. Only consciousness can add information and direct evolution. Therefore consciousness is the cause of evolution and not a product of evolution. What has evolved is not consciousness but the means for its expression through brain contained in BMI complex. Consciousness is not a product of BMI complex but its producer. And consciousness belongs to soul.

The relationship between BMI complex and soul is poetically described by Sri. Krishna in Bhagavad Gita as that of a garment and the wearer of the garment. BMI complex is the garment and the soul is the wearer of the garment. We should realize that we are not the garments but the wearer of the garment. **The wearer of the garment is more important than the garment one wears.**

All our personalities—father, son, doctor, executive etc. as well as our BMI complex—are what we wear and not what we are. What we are is intrinsic and what we have is incidental. What we are is more important than what we have. What we have is for our use. We have to learn to use what we have appropriately to be happy. This can only happen when we have a clear knowledge of what we are and what we have.

6

Law of Causation

In the previous chapter it was pointed out that what we are is the soul (*Atma)* and everything else other than soul (*Atma*) is called *anAtma*. Soul is what we are and *anatma* is what we use as our equipment for our transactions. An equipment properly used is a blessing; an improperly used one can result in a disaster. To properly use the equipment we should be thoroughly familiar with its mode of operation. For instance if we know how to operate an automobile it will take us to our desired destination. If we do not know how to handle the automobile properly we will face disastrous consequences. To handle the equipment of *anatma* we should gain a thorough knowledge of its mode of functioning.

The phenomenal world we live in is nothing but a series of causes and effects. In the chain of cause and effect each link serves both as a cause and as an effect. The distinguishing feature between cause and effect is temporal. Cause precedes the effect. For instance water evaporates from the oceans and condenses at higher levels of the atmosphere to become clouds. Water from oceans is the cause of clouds. Clouds which are an effect then become the cause of rain—the effect. Rain water the effect of clouds then becomes the cause for vegetation to grow and the chain continues. The relationship between cause and effect is not random but is governed and regulated by physical, chemical, biological, psychological, moral, and many other laws. These laws are infallible, invariable, and impersonal. A mango seed infallibly will produce only a mango tree and not an oak tree. Water at sea level invariably boils at 100 degrees centigrade. We cannot make it boil at less than that temperature. And it boils at 100 degrees centigrade regardless of age, gender, nationality or religious affiliation of a person boiling the water. Furthermore no matter whoever transgresses the law knowingly or unknowingly will have to pay a penalty. When two speeding cars collide, the cars get damaged. We call it an accident. As a matter of fact there are no accidents. All the so called accidents are the result of disobedience to a particular law. The damage resulting from collision of two speeding cars is due to infringement of the physical law that two things cannot occupy the same space at the same time. The relationship between a cause and its effect is called law of causation.

The infallibility, invariability, and impersonal nature of these laws have their own advantages. Because of their predictability we can confidently plan an action to obtain a desired result. Imagine what havoc it would have been if water were to boil one day at 100 degrees centigrade and on another day freeze at that temperature. Under such unpredictable conditions planning becomes an impossibility. Under such circumstances we could not be sure of even getting our first cup of morning coffee! Another important aspect of these laws is that they are discoverable by adequate effort on our part. When we discover the laws we get empowered and we can make our lives better provided we use them wisely. At one time we did not know what caused a disease like the dreaded smallpox. It was considered to be a visitation from God as a punishment for our sins of commissions and omissions. However the discovery of smallpox virus as the cause of the dreaded disease removed all our misunderstandings about the disease and enabled us to treat as well as prevent it. Today the once dreaded disease is eradicated from the surface of the earth. This is an example of using a discovery wisely. The same discovery may be misused for waging biological warfare to the detriment of humanity. With the passage of time we have discovered an increasing number of these laws. Consequently many events previously considered mysterious or miracles can now be explained on a rational basis.

Because of the various laws the complex vast universe of ours is maintained and is operating smoothly and seamlessly as an organic whole. If we describe creation as a product which is intelligently put together then the universe satisfies that definition. Intelligence behind the creation becomes obvious even by a cursory examination. Nothing is redundant in this universe. Everything serves a purpose. We breathe out carbon dioxide which is poisonous to us. Plants require carbon dioxide to synthesize carbohydrates and other food products and in the process give out oxygen we need. There is perfect balance and in this process both plants and animals benefit by their interdependence. It is a win-win situation. Our own body is a wonderful example of an intelligent creation. Trillions of individual cells in our body function for the welfare of the whole body in perfect harmony. Organisms are organized objects both structurally and functionally exhibiting hierarchical order, differentiation, interaction of innumerable processes and goal directed behavior. Even the so called primitive unicellular organisms have an incredibly elaborate array of highly structured organelles each with its own metabolic function. The more we come to know of the biological processes even at the unicellular organism level it becomes more and more difficult to explain it on a purely mechanistic basis. Only intelligence guidance can explain such observed facts.

It is our experience that every creation requires a creator endowed with intelligence. For instance a carpenter is required for the creation of furniture. Human beings endowed with intelligence perceived universe as a creation and therefore deduced that it must have a creator and the creator was given the name God. However God as an object is not available for our perception. Therefore knowledge and attributes concerning God have remained speculative. Being a creator, God is considered to be sentient since insentient objects lack power of creation. It is our experience that a creator of an object possesses knowledge of what he creates, skills to create and resources at his disposal for his creation. God, the creator of this limitless universe should have limitless knowledge, skills and resources. Being limitless God can only be one, since two limitless entities cannot logically exist. God, therefore, must be one. However concepts concerning God are many. Two concepts concerning God will be dealt with here because of their bearing on happiness.

Anthropomorphic God

Since God is not an object of our perception knowledge and attributes concerning God are speculative. It is our experience that a creator of an object is a sentient being possessing knowledge of what he creates, skill to create it and resources available for his creation. Therefore God the creator of the entire universe must be all knowing, all powerful and must have at his disposal all resources. It is also our experience that the creator and the product of his creation are two separate entities like the potter who is separate from the pots he creates. So God is considered to be different from his creation—the universe—and separate from it. Such reasoning led to the concept of an anthropomorphic God with highly magnified human qualities. The concept of an anthropomorphic God has its advantages. We all face problems in life. We like to have someone to share our difficulty, help overcome it and relieve our mind of worry and anxiety. But there may not be people available for us who are either interested in or capable of solving our problems. Concept of a merciful, kind, powerful, loving, always available personal God is a source of great solace and strength when faced with adverse situations. Religions do portray God in this image and expect us to believe this concept on the basis of faith. Such a faith based concept of God raises the question, "How an almighty, compassionate God did not create a more perfect world full of happiness? Why there is so much misery in this world? Why so many horrible things do happen?" Therefore some conclude that belief in God is for fools and consider themselves as rational and do not want to believe in the existence of God. When someone proclaims that he does not believe in God what that person means is that he does not believe in his own concept of a personal merciful, powerful God. What is rational is to align our concepts to suit the facts. It is not rational to expect the facts to change to suit our concepts. What is required to be rational is not faith based belief in God but an understanding of God. A belief is an acceptance of something as true until proved otherwise. Once a belief is verified and is found to be true, it ceases to be a belief and becomes a fact. A fact is based on knowledge; a belief on faith. Faith may be shaken but not knowledge. For instance, you have knowledge that fire burns. If the whole world were to tell you that fire is cold, you would disagree with courage and conviction and you will not touch fire. Such courage and conviction, however, would be lacking in a belief.

Beliefs are either verifiable or non-verifiable. When an astronomer says that a galaxy exists 1000 light years away from us there is no reason for not believing it since a knowledgeable person without any ulterior motive has provided this information. In addition, there is a methodology to verify the information given to us by the astronomer, if we so desired. This is an example of a verifiable belief. On the other hand, belief in heaven is non-verifiable. Its existence can neither be proved nor disproved. There is no scope of settling the issue of existence or nonexistence of heaven by either the believers or nonbelievers.

Even for a non-verifiable belief to be viable it should not be opposed to reason. That good people will find a place in heaven is a viable non-verifiable belief. However a belief that entry into heaven is possible only for members of a particular sect regardless of their conduct is opposed to reason and not viable. If God were to limit entry to heaven by that criterion, he would be a sectarian God, not a universal God. He is the creator; His relationship to all human beings is the same, namely, He is the creator and we are all created. We expect our earthly parents to treat all their children equally. So how can we accept that our father in heaven to be partial to a particular sect? Such a concept is opposed to reason. A belief that is opposed to reason creates confusion. And to live with confusion is uncomfortable and a source of unhappiness. Confusion can be cleared only by aligning our beliefs with reason.

Assuming that God is almighty, why should he be compassionate to us? Is it because we want him to be so? We want him as a compassionate being taking personal interest in us for our benefit. Are we his masters to dictate terms as to how He should treat us? Is it possible for God to be compassionate in accordance with our narrow vision? Suppose two football teams are playing against each other, and each prays for victory. Could God favor both with victory? Of course not. If he were to favor one team over the other, he would be accused of partiality. If he were to be partial, he would be no better than ordinary mortals.

We live not in one but in two creations. One is God's creation and the other is our own creation. God's creation is intelligent. It is governed and sustained by invariable, impartial, and infallible physical, chemical, biological and other laws. In God's creation there are only events, neither good nor bad, all governed by laws. We, however, look at the events through the biased view of our own likes and dislikes. An event we like makes us happy and we label it as good. An event we dislike makes us unhappy and we label it as bad. The labels are designated by us. What is good for one may be bad for another and vice versa. Birth and death, for example, are biological events. From our point of view birth is considered "good" and death is "bad." Furthermore our concept of good and bad keeps changing and is not constant. For example, death will be viewed differently depending on circumstances. During war death of an enemy soldier will be considered as good whereas death of our own soldiers will be considered as bad. Therefore it is not possible to make laws which makes everyone all the time happy. Moreover if God were to keep on changing the laws governing this universe to satisfy the whims and fancies of everyone, there would be nothing but chaos. There will be no predictability. Without predictability life becomes miserable. Because the laws are invariable, impartial, and infallible we have the branch of knowledge we call science benefiting us. We cannot change these laws, but we can understand these laws and can take advantage of them for our benefit. For example, a pilot who jumps from an aircraft cannot change the law of gravity to avoid the harmful effects of the impact. But he can use a parachute for soft landing. Physical laws dictate the occurrence of such events as hurricanes, earthquakes, and tornadoes. In 1980, scientists were able to predict the volcanic eruption of Mount St. Helens in Washington State based on their knowledge of volcanic eruptions. Forewarned, people were able to stay out of harm's way and enjoyed the spectacle. On the other hand if we were ignorant of the laws of volcanic eruptions people would have stayed in harm's way and there would have been loss of lives as well as property damage. Then the volcano would have been viewed as a disaster instead of as a natural spectacle. Indeed, all our technological progress is the result of understanding the laws and taking advantage of them. The concept of a personal almighty compassionate God and the suffering we encounter in this world is mutually incompatible.

The concept of God as an anthropomorphic entity is beset with additional problems. Religions have played a major role in defining God for the lay public. The different concepts of God, by different religions, are like the proverbial description of an elephant by four blind men each describing it as a rope, a pillar, a wall, and a fan. The blind men were not wrong in their description but their vision was incomplete. Unfortunately the incomplete vision of God presented by different religions has produced bitter conflicts including bloodshed among people of different religions each claiming the superiority of their own concept of God.

The anthropomorphic conception of God, the lowest level of presentation of God, has logical fallacies. With maturity questions as to what material God used for creation, from where and how He got it arise. How a limited anthropomorphic being can have unlimited features to create this limitless universe? In answer to these questions concept of God was taken to a higher level by ancient Hindu sages.

Not One God but Only God

It is our experience that for any creation we need both the intelligent and material cause. For creation of furniture the carpenter is the intelligent cause and wood is the material cause. In the anthropomorphic concept of God, God is presented as the intelligent cause of creation. The question as to the origin of the material cause was left unanswered. The sages figured that to be logical God should both be the intelligent and the material cause of the universe. The analogy of spider, which gets the material from itself for the creation of its web, is advanced to understand the concept of God both as the intelligent and the material cause of the universe. This concept is a breakthrough in the evolution of human thought and has important corollaries including:

1. The whole of the creation, including us, is an organic whole. In other words we are an inseparable integral part of the whole and not separate independent entities.

2. The distinction between the sacred and the secular ceases to exist. Everything becomes sacred. Such an attitude necessities treating our fellow human beings, animals, plants, our own BMI complex and even non-living objects with care, consideration, and with a prayerful attitude paving the way for a harmonious happier life.

3. The material cause is not away from its product just as gold is not away from gold ornaments. All forms of ornaments are sustained by gold alone. The essence of all gold ornaments is gold. Similarly all forms we see in this universe are God's forms. Therefore there is no superior or inferior form. Privilege is the bane of human existence resulting from concept of superiority and inferiority. The concept that no one is superior and no one is inferior is a powerful antidote for the problems caused by privilege seeking behavior.

4. The glory we see in any and every object belongs to God. This should make us humble and is a powerful antidote for jealousy and other negative tendencies which rob us of our happiness.

One may not believe in God as portrayed by religions. Such a belief is not even necessary. We may dismiss God from our concept. But we can neither dismiss the existence of laws governing this universe nor intelligence behind the creation. These laws were not authored by us. We are subject to these laws without escape. It is our subjectivity in the form of our biases which prevents us from being in conformity with the laws of creation and causing us to be unhappy. When our actions are not in accordance with the law of causation we will be rubbing against the laws causing friction. The friction results in unhappiness. The more objective we are the greater will be our conformity with laws of creation and our happiness.

Part 2

udyamena hi sidhyanti kAryaNi na manorathai.
nahi suptasya simhasya pravishanti mukhe mrugAh.
(Success is attained only by effort and not by day dreaming.
No deer voluntarily enters the mouth of a sleeping lion.)

In order to achieve an object of our desire knowledge about the objet, while necessary, is not sufficient. To gain the object of desire we have to put effort. In order to feed itself a lion has to hunt. Its hunger is not quenched by knowledge of hunting alone. No deer voluntarily enters the mouth of a lion to quench its hunger. Hunting requires effort on the part of the lion. Similarly to be happy we have to bring about a cognitive change resulting in a life of objectivity, nonviolence, accommodation, integrity, a sense of not owning anything. With constant effort on our part we will be able to gain victory over our internal enemies responsible for our unhappiness and remain happy.

7

Reap as You Sow

We know from our experience that some people are born with a silver spoon in their mouth and others not even a properly functioning mouth. Such a state of affairs appears unfair and unjust. The question arises as to what is responsible for such a sorry state of affairs in which some are happy and others unhappy. Is man a helpless victim to the whims and fancies of some tyrannical force with no escape? Or is there any hope to shape one's life with self effort? Are there laws which govern such occurrences? If there are laws accounting for such disparities can they be discovered? Can we benefit from the knowledge of such laws for improving our lives just as we have done in other fields for our happiness?

Such disparities we observe are attributed to fate. But attributing happy or unhappy situations of individuals to fate does not explain anything and is of no help. The question still remains as to what is responsible for fate. What is important is that we should become masters of our fate and not its slaves.

There are two closely related laws of causation applicable to humans. They are the law of destiny and law of *karma*. The law of destiny connects our past to our present status. Law of *karma* is much more comprehensive and it deals with our present, past, and future. Knowledge of these laws, when put to practice, will influence our state of happiness.

Law of Destiny

What we are at present is the cumulative effect of all our previous thoughts, desires and actions. Our past activity is the cause and our present is the effect. Our present is our destiny. Whatever has happened in the past has happened and it cannot be changed. It is like an arrow which has been released from a bow. Once released, the arrow will take its own course. Our past is a choice-less situation and like all choice-less situations leaves no choice other than accepting it. The very fact of confronting and accepting the past paves the way for liberation from guilt, anger, greed, jealousy and other negative aspects of our personality. The greater we resist acceptance of negativity in our past the greater will be our unhappiness. Our present destiny is the result of our past actions. **In other words we are responsible for what we are and none else.** Therefore it is neither fair nor beneficial to blame anyone else for our present status. We have to take responsibility. It is a hard task indeed!

Law of Karma

Law of karma is a logical extension of law of destiny and is based on the principle of the relationship between cause and effect. The law covers our past, present, and our future. According to law of *karma* we are not only the product of our past actions but also the producers of our own future. If our past actions have decided our present, logically our present actions would determine our future. We are both a product and a producer at the same time; product from the point of the past and producer from the point of future. There is a misconception that law of karma is pessimistic and fatalistic. It is neither. It only makes a statement of fact. **The law provides us an opportunity to learn from our past and infuses with optimism about our future while emphasizing the importance of self effort in the present.** We are bound no doubt by our past but are free to act in shaping our future. We are both bound and free at the same time. Our situation can be compared to that of a game of cards. What cards we get is comparable to destiny and how we use those cards to our self effort in trying to determine the outcome of the game. In the present we are free to choose our actions. Noble thoughts and good actions on our part will be processed by the laws of causation and will be returned to us in the form of a happier life. Bad thoughts and bad actions will have the opposite effect. **But once we choose our actions we will be subject to their positive as well as negative consequences. There is no escape.**

There are two forces shaping our lives, namely, destiny and self effort. Some people attach importance to self effort and others to destiny. Our future destiny will be the result of the net influence of both of them. They may work additively or in opposition. The following is an example to illustrate the effect of their net contribution. Imagine a river flowing at 10 miles per hour (destiny). A swimmer enters the river and can swim at two miles per hour (self effort). If he decides to swim along the flow of the river he will cover 12 (10 +2) miles in one hour. If he decides to swim against the current he will cover (10-2) 8 miles in one hour. The net effect is determined by the interaction between destiny and self effort.

Our situation is comparable to that of an animal tied to a post with a long rope. The animal is not free to roam about anywhere it wants. Neither is it totally lacking freedom. Within the limits allowed by the rope it can do what it desires. It may walk, run, sit or sleep. Each of us has to work out our destiny within the bounds of the laws governing this universe taking full responsibility for the choices we make.

When we talk about the results of past actions, they are not confined to that of our present life but extend to innumerable past lives. Our present life is only one in the series of lives centered on our soul. Our soul has taken many different bodies evolving to higher states of consciousness with the passage of time.

In the concept of reincarnation people are responsible for their own salvation. If an individual is responsible for his own destiny then there will be no need for dependence on priests for one's salvation. Believers in reincarnation are neither amenable to conversion as faithful followers by promises of heavenly pleasures nor intimidated by suffering in hell. In other words belief in reincarnation is a threat to the power of priests over the masses. Therefore it was in the interest of priests not to endorse belief in reincarnation. So in some religions the concept of reincarnation was discouraged. However in Hinduism, Buddhism, Jainism, and Sikhism belief in reincarnation is accepted.

There are people who consider reincarnation a wooly concept invented for our solace as an explanation for the disparities we encounter in this world. However many mind boggling difficulties can be resolved by a proper understanding of the concept of reincarnation. In our universe both at the micro and macro level everything is subject to cycle of birth, death, and rebirth. At macro level we know planets and galaxies are born and they die giving birth to new planets and galaxies. At the micro level the particles that constitute atoms are interacting with each other undergoing annihilation and regeneration. Everything in the universe is paradoxically destructible and yet indestructible at the same time; dead yet very alive. This phenomenon is what is to be understood as reincarnation. We know from our scientific knowledge that matter and energy are inter-convertible. Neither matter nor energy can be created nor destroyed. They undergo different manifestations. Our physical body is the product of millions of years of evolution. However evolution is not confined to our physical form only. Our soul is in the process of spiritual evolution. It has a prehuman past and a superhuman future. There is wide variation among humans in their degree of spiritual evolution ranging from a human brute to a human angel. Just as successive years are needed for our physical development, successions of lives are needed for our spiritual development. For spiritual evolution we have to learn certain lessons and pass certain tests. When we have not learnt the lessons or have failed to live in accordance with the laws governing the universe our soul is granted another opportunity to learn and grow with a new physical body.

Certain phenomenon such as instances of past life memories, phobias, child prodigies, successful treatment of certain physical and medical ailments by past life therapy, and xenoglossia (speaking in a language unknown/unfamiliar to the speaker) are best explained by reincarnation. One objection raised against the concept of reincarnation is, "Why everyone does not remember past lives?" Recollection of memory of past lives requires activation. It happens in some instances spontaneously. When not spontaneous it can be activated under hypnosis, if so desired. It is worth remembering that it is nature's kindness that we have amnesia for our past lives. For many of us the memories of our present life itself is a tremendous burden to carry. The added load of memories of our previous births will become an intolerable burden to bear. Memory of our past lives could make living in our present birth too stressful. We should count our blessing for lack of memory of past lives. Moreover memory as a basis for validating the existence of reincarnation is flawed. We do not have memory of many events in our present life such as our birth and our early childhood. Nonetheless no one can deny their occurrence.

There are attempts made to explain differences in personality on the basis of genetics. If genetics was totally responsible for the differences then identical twins should have the same personality which is not always the case. One may argue that the differences between the personalities of identical twins are due to environmental factors. However conjoint twins not only share the same genes but also same environment. There are reports of conjoint twins having different personalities despite the commonality of their genes and environmental influences. This observation can be explained by the presence of two different souls at different levels of spiritual progress manifesting as two personalities. Physical body is only a medium for the interaction of soul with the world and the interaction is determined by the uniqueness of each soul.

There are many advantages to be gained from the concept of reincarnation. Concept of reincarnation relieves the misapprehension that few days or years is an entire life time. It points out that human existence is much vaster, grander and carries greater meaning and purpose. **It makes us responsible for what we are and what we could be.**

Once upon a time a famer lived in a village and he had a horse to help him with his chores. One day the horse ran away and could not be found. His neighbors said. "It is because of your bad luck the horse ran away."

The farmer replied, "May be."

Few days later the horse returned with another horse. The farmer had two horses instead of one. His neighbors said, "It was because of your good luck you got two horses."

The farmer said, "May be."

While the farmer's son was trying to train the new horse he fell and broke his leg. The neighbors said, "It is because of bad luck that your son broke his leg."

The farmer true to his practice said, "May be."

While the son was convalescing from his injury king's men came to the village to conscript all the young men for the army for fighting an impending war. However the farmer's son was spared because of injuries. The villagers said that the famer was lucky to have his son spared from military duty. What looks as good or bad in isolation may have different connotation when viewed as a part of the whole. Similarly what may look as unfair or unjust when viewed from the point of a single life span may be viewed differently when taken into consideration several lives. Only through many lives can the various experiences could be properly understood in broader perspective. What may appear as unjust or unfair when viewed from the narrow perspective of a single life may look just when viewed in the context of several lives. Words like "fate," "accident," "coincidence" lose their significance when an individual accepts that only he is responsible for all the experiences. Reincarnation gives the hope and solace that we are on a journey to perfection and every experience is for our advancement and not to be resented.

Concept of reincarnation when internalized can profoundly change our lives for the better not only as individuals but of the whole humanity. How can anyone harm or harbor prejudice against the kind of person one has been or will be especially if one has to face retribution in a future life? It provides the moral basis for shaping one's life. Naturally we become gentler and more understanding of others in our dealings with them—a prerequisite for a harmonious happier life.

Even if we are ignorant of a law, so long as we do not transgress it, we do not get penalized. For instance monkeys living on tree tops do not know law of gravity. However they know that so long as they hold on to the branches of the tree they are safe from falling and do not get hurt. On the other hand when a law is transgressed, even if one is aware of it, a penalty has to be paid. A professor of gravity will not be spared from getting hurt if he were to fall from a height. What we know or do not know is secondary. What is important is whether we are adhering to the law or not. Adherence to the laws, even in the absence of knowledge of their existence, will be sufficient to ensure our survival. However to prosper and not be satisfied with mere survival the laws have to be understood. Understanding these laws requires a prepared mind. Apples were falling from trees for many years. It was the prepared mind of Newton which understood the significance of this occurrence that discovered the law of gravity. Empowered by the knowledge of gravity we were able to figure out the precise force required for launching a vehicle into outer space for exploring the vast universe. Knowledge of reincarnation and its application in our lives can launch us to a higher level of consciousness for enjoying greater happiness.

8

No Pain No Gain

We all want to be happy. In the previous chapter we saw that we are responsible for our own happiness. No goal in life can be achieved without proper preparation and effort on our part. Happiness is no exception to this rule. Unfortunately we do not achieve our goal by desiring but by making ourselves deserving of what we desire. For instance it takes no effort to desire to eat a delicious meal but it takes lot of time and effort to prepare it before it can be enjoyed.

It has been previously made clear that happiness is not in the outside world; happiness is inside us. Indeed happiness is our nature. During moments of happiness we are established in our true nature. Happiness is a state of pleased mind free from sense of limitation. It is in being rather than in becoming. Happiness is where there is no seeking. Happiness is where the seeker-sought divide is resolved. Since happiness is our true nature all we need to do is claim our true nature.

What Prevents Us from Claiming Our True Nature?

Happiness is our natural state and unhappiness is a disruption of the natural state. For us to be happy what is needed is we should prevent its disruption. In our misguided belief that happiness is something to be achieved we disrupt our own happiness. To be happy what we have to do is to remove those factors that are obscuring our understanding of our true nature. For eliminating the obscuring factors we need to bring about a cognitive change in ourselves. It is said that our beliefs become our thoughts; our thoughts become our words; our words become our actions; our actions become our habits; our habits become our values; and our values become our destiny. Therefore our journey should begin with the belief that happiness is our true nature.

The world consists of mineral, vegetable, animal and human kingdoms. Minerals grossly appear inert. However each mineral at the atomic level is different from one another. There is activity within the atoms of the minerals in the form of movement. Minerals undergo physical and chemical changes. However they lack the capacity for self expression. In the vegetable kingdom we see more activity in the form of growth and movement. However the motion we see in plant kingdom is confined to one dimension. They have limited power to move from place to place. Animals are more conscious compared to plants. Their motion is not confined to one spot. They can travel great distances if a need were to arise. Among the animals humans are the most evolved. They exhibit greater energy and consciousness compared to other animals.

Human beings vary widely in their degree of self centeredness. At one end of the spectrum are those who are not removed too far from beasts. They are gross, lethargic and consumed in sense gratification even at the cost of their kith and kin. At the opposite end of the spectrum are the human angels having no trace of selfishness. Such men are rare. They represent human perfection. They embrace everyone regardless of caste, color, nationality as their own. Their compassion extends not only to fellow human beings but to all creatures under the sun. They live not as isolated individuals separate from the totality of existence but as an integral inseparable part of the creation which is an organic whole. They see themselves in everything and everything in themselves. In that state there is nothing to be feared or desired. By progressively identifying with our higher personality our lower impulses and tendencies get sublimated. Our goal should be to progressively move on to become divine persons just as a river reaches the ocean overcoming all obstacles during the course of its flow.

Suppose we were to land on Mars and a person there were to ask us, "Where are you from?" More than likely we would answer, "We are from earth." Suppose if we are from America and are visiting India and if we were asked, "Where are you from?" We would answer, "We are from America." If we are Americans living in New York and are visiting San Francisco for the question, "Where are you from?" we will reply, "We are from New York." If another resident of New York were to ask us, "Where are you from?" we may answer that we are from Bronx etc. depending on the borough of our residence. In Bronx we may identify ourselves with a street and in a street to a particular house depending on further questioning. When we identify ourselves with a particular house in Bronx we have become exclusive and we become more and more inclusive as we progress in the opposite direction to our identification with earth. When we identify ourselves with earth it includes, America, New York, Bronx and the street and the house in Bronx. But when we identify with a house in Bronx there is no doubt earth is in Bronx but Bronx is not earth. Our thinking and actions are influenced by our inclusivity or exclusivity. Religious leaders like Krishna, Buddha, and Christ were inclusive and hence are revered whereas despots like Hitler, Stalin etc. are despised because of their exclusivity. In inclusivity there is harmony and in exclusivity strife. No one likes strife—a source of unhappiness. We have the choice of moving towards inclusivity or exclusivity.

We are made up of the same great elements—space, air, fire, water and earth—in common with the rest of the universe. The solidity we experience of our body is only a notion. The elements in our body are in constant exchange with rest of the elements in the creation which is a manifestation of existence. We are different from moment to moment because of this exchange. We do not have the same body moment to moment. At times we will have some of the oxygen molecules which great persons like Gandhi, Lincoln and others had in their bodies. At other times we will have the oxygen molecules of people like Hitler, Stalin, and other despots had. It is also possible there may be combination of oxygen molecules of great men and despots at the same time in our body. The solidity of our physical body is due to a state of dynamic equilibrium between the body and the rest of the creation. Our body is a little continuously changing aggregation of matter in an unbroken ocean of matter. Physically we are, therefore, an integral part of the whole creation and not separate from it. We are part and parcel of the creation which is an organic whole. At the physical level we share one universe. At the chemical level we share one pattern of metabolism. Thousands of chemical reactions take place in our body and many of these reactions are common to all living beings including plants. At biological level we share one life. At social level we are one humanity. Our limited individual consciousness is like a little whirlpool in the river of one cosmic consciousness. The concept of oneness of existence and that we are part and parcel of that one existence when assimilated will have tremendous implications. Only by assimilation of the fact of oneness of existence[1] including ourselves can we get over the sense of limitations we suffer in comparison to what we are not. A drop of water if it had human qualities would feel very limited, insecure and unhappy. However if it merges in the ocean it is not destroyed but loses its sense of limitation. Similarly only by identifying ourselves with existence which is an organic whole we can get over our sense of insecurity and resultant unhappiness arising from our clinging to our notion as separate, independent individual entities. A spiritual man is one who has succeeded in merging his individual self in the totality of existence. This state is what religion means by the concept of regaining grace of God. For this transformation to occur a cognitive change is needed on our part. And the information about our true nature gained at the intellectual level must result in transformation. Transformation must be reflected in our actions for a happier life. Our ego or individuality which is responsible for our sense of separation from the rest of the creation resists the needed cognitive change. This is understandable since such a change results in annihilation of ego and naturally ego resists its own annihilation making the transformation difficult. The task before us is to tame our ego. The task is hard but the rewards are great.

---

[1] When we say a table exists, I exist, you exist, space exists, matter exists, energy exists etc., what is common to all of the objects is existence. All objects are nothing but different manifestations of one unbroken existence.

9

Taming of the Ego
Part I
Practice

The importance of a cognitive change for our happiness was discussed in the previous chapter. Even to realize that a cognitive change is needed for our happiness is by itself a major step in the right direction. Sri Krishna points out in Bhagavad Gita (7:3 and 7: 19) that rare is the person who tries to bring about a change in one's orientation and still rarer is the person who succeeds. However Krishna's observation should not lead us to despair. He himself suggests the means for bringing about the needed cognitive change. The means include constant practice (*abhyAsa*) and maintaining objectivity (*vairAgya*).

It was previously pointed out that the state of happiness is comparable to silence. Noise is a violation of silence. Silence ensues as soon we stop disturbing it by making noise. To create silence nothing more needs to be done. Similarly to be happy we should stop violating it by unhappiness. Unhappiness is the enemy to be subdued. To subdue an enemy a prerequisite is an accurate knowledge of his location. To eliminate unhappiness violating our happiness we have to first locate the source of unhappiness. Let us begin our investigation with our physical personality which is the grossest of our personalities. Physical body has no capacity to do anything on its own. It is just a machine like an automobile. An automobile has no destination of its own. It is the driver who has a destination. The automobile serves the driver as his tool for reaching his destination. Automobile totally subserves the purpose of the driver and has no independent action of its own. So too, the body is an instrument under the control of an "individual" or the "thinker."

Sense organs only report existence of objects in the external world to the mind. They are just the carriers of information to mind and nothing more. Mind receives the information from sense organs and integrates the information. The integrated information becomes a thought in the mind. Mind is nothing but a flow of thoughts. For an object to affect us it must be in the form of a thought in our mind. When there is no thought of an object in our mind that object cannot affect us. That is why strangers, who are not present in our thought, are no problem for us. On the contrary people we know are in our thought and we have problems with them.

Thoughts are our impressions of our perception. They provide us knowledge. A thought is knowledge in relation to a particular object or an experience. Knowledge as such is not a problem for us. It only becomes a problem for us when another thought which says, "I want it" or "I do not want it" is added on to it. There are so many products in the world we are aware of such as shoes, dress, automobiles etc. The knowledge of these objects is not a problem. But the moment the "I want it" thought makes its appearance in our mind our problem begins. It creates a division of the seeker and the sought. The "I want it" thought progressively becomes stronger and stronger and tension builds up within us to obtain the object. We remain unhappy and dissatisfied with ourselves until the object is gained. There is always the possibility of not gaining the object for various reasons. The thought that we may not gain the object makes us anxious. When there are many contenders for the same desired object there ensues competition. The other competitors are looked upon as a hindrance in gaining the desired object and resentment sets in. With resentment the division between "I" against "them" becomes unavoidable. This situation further reinforces our individual identity separate from the rest of the creation.

We should not lose sight of the fact that no object is a problem for us by itself. We all possess few things. There are many things we do not possess. In fact the things that we do not possess far exceed in number the things we do posses. The absence of things we do not possess makes no difference for us and do not disturb us in the least so long as we are indifferent towards them. However when we consider an object worth possessing then a certain pattern of thinking ensues. Initially we start missing the object. We feel incomplete and dissatisfied with ourselves (*apurNa*). This dissatisfaction is the result of our intellectual conclusion that the object is worthy of possession and with it we will be happy. This is wrong thinking since no external object has happiness as an attribute. Such misguided thinking that external objects make us happy is delusion (*moha*). The more we dwell on the object of desire the thought of gaining the object becomes stronger and stronger. So long as the object is not possessed we feel discontented and unhappy. The discontentment gets released only after possessing the desired object. When the urge to get the desired object is very strong we may even resort to immoral and illegal means. It is important to realize that no object ever forced us to take it. No object has such a power. The object by which we were attracted was not an attraction for many others. No object in our possession ever told us, "Take me home with you." We took them along with us by our own sweet will. It is we who were responsible for the thinking that we are incomplete without that object and we will be happy only after gaining that object. The object is neutral. It has neither joy nor sorrow to give us. It is our pattern of thinking in relation to an object which makes the difference. If a certain pattern of our thinking is responsible for our discontentment with ourselves then we are the problem. We can become the solution by changing our pattern of thinking. **We are the problem and we are the solution.**

No object is a seducer for us. Neither an object nor thought of an object is a problem for us. It is the thinker in the form of "I" thought and its extension "mine" which creates the problem. The following analogy will help in our understanding. We all need food for our survival. The need for food will be signaled by hunger. With a bowl of rice or a few pieces of bread hunger subsides and the physical body is satisfied. The body would stop eating when hunger is quenched, a phenomenon well seen in animals. However mind even after hunger has subsided whispers, "Have one more dessert. It is very tasty." We should not lose sight of the fact that it is only a suggestion. What the mind is telling us is a suggestion and not a command for us to eat. A suggestion by itself is not a problem. A suggestion may be accepted or rejected. A suggestion is only one of the choices among many. Unfortunately many of us take the suggestion as a command. A command leaves no choice. Command demands obedience. The problem is we obediently follow the suggestion as a command. We do not fully understand and appreciate the difference between a suggestion and a command. Consequently we become slaves to our mind.

If we have to escape from this slavery we have to clearly understand the difference between "getting a thought" and learning to think. Suppose our mind whispers to us "Have a candy." At this stage it is only a suggestion. We have the option of following the suggestion, rejecting the suggestion or doing something else other than the suggestion. For choosing one of the three options we have to be there as a thinker deciding what is best under the circumstances. Then we will be masters of our mind and not its slaves. To take a deliberate decision when mind makes a suggestion we should be alert. Then only we can say we are thinking. Unfortunately what happens more often than not is that we succumb to mind's suggestion. We own up the suggestion, make it our own, nurture it and become slaves to it. We then delude ourselves as thinkers. We are not acting as thinkers. We have allowed our minds to take many liberties with us over a long period of time. Mind likes to continue enjoying the liberties it is used to and naturally it resists being disciplined. **But we have to be constantly alert to assert our role as masters over our mind.** We should always remember that mind is a good servant but a bad master. We have to establish proper healthy relationship with our mind. A struggle is inevitable. In the struggle, especially in the early stages, setbacks are the rule rather than the exception. Nevertheless we should persevere in bringing the mind under our control. This requires repeated effort on our part. This is what constitutes practice (*abhyAsa*).

Changes in our pattern of thinking occur gradually. It is like climbing a staircase. We progress from one step to the next. With each step we make progress and to that extent we get benefited. No effort goes to waste. With each effort our ability to effectively handle ourselves and the world increases. We become efficient in our day to day life in dealing with our profession, family, and friends resulting in incremental increase in our happiness. The gain is well worth the effort.

10

Taming of the Mind
Part II
Objectivity

If we were to watch a lake we will see waves on its surface. The waves make their appearance, last for some time, and then disappear. The movement of water which we see as waves will create patterns in the sand on the floor of the lake which are not easily visible to us. These patterns in the sand on the floor of the lake are more enduring than the waves which created them. Our thoughts are comparable to waves and every thought contributes to the formation of an impression (*vAsana*) comparable to the patterns created in the sand on the floor of the lake. These impressions remain dormant in our mind. The thoughts that arise in our mind have their origin in the accumulated pool of impressions. Thus impressions and thoughts are inter-related and influence one another.

As previously pointed out mind is nothing but a flow of thoughts. A thought may arise from the pool of our accumulated impressions (*vAsana*) spontaneously or be triggered from an object or an event. We have no control as to what thought may arises in our mind at any given moment.

Therefore we are not responsible for a thought that arises from the pool of impressions (*vAsanAh*). However we have the choice in dealing with the thought with our free will. **Therefore we are responsible what we do with a thought and its consequences.**

Mahatma Gandhi was thrown out of a train in apartheid South Africa by a white ticket collector for travelling in a first class compartment even though he had a valid ticket for the journey. His initial response was anger. With anger he could have nurtured thoughts of taking revenge over the white race for the injustice meted out to him based on his skin color. However he thought about the situation and decided to change the mindset of the white men. He decided to make them aware of their wrong thinking and the resulting injustice to fellow human beings. His aim was not to destroy the white men but to destroy their wrong thinking. The choice he made in handling his thoughts has profoundly influenced the world in a positive fashion. In contrast Hitler for whatever perceived injustice done to him by the Jews sent several millions of them to gas chambers. A positive emotion like love leads us on the path to divinity whereas negative emotions degrade us to become devils.

Thoughts are powerful and have great energy. They can be constructive or destructive. They can help or hinder us in our development depending on how we use them. We human beings have the potential to become divine or devilish. Which potential we exploit depends on how we manage our thoughts. Our world consists not only of objects in the external world but also thoughts and emotions in our inner world of mind. We do not see the world as it is. We see a world filtered through the prism of our biases, cultural conditioning, past experiences and consideration of personal gain or loss. World seen through the prism of our biases etc. is a subjective world.

On the contrary a world seen free from the intervening prism of our biases etc. is an objective world. For thoughts to become creative and benefit us, we should become objective in their management. Our subjectivity or objectivity will have important implications on our behavior and for our happiness. Some examples of subjectivity and objectivity will help us in better understanding their implications.

We are very objective when dealing with fire. We know that it is the nature of fire to burn. We also know we cannot change the burning property of fire. So we accept fire as it is and make use of that property of fire for our advantage. If we accidentally burn ourselves with fire we do not blame the fire or hate it. We decide to be more careful in the future to avoid being burnt. Objectivity is the doorway to avoid disappointments and consequent unhappiness.

Two people started a business as partners. At the end of the year they made a profit of 10 per cent on their investment. One of the partners who had expected 15 per cent profit was unhappy. On the other hand the partner who had expected 5 per cent profit was ecstatic. The profit was the same in terms of money for both partners—10 per cent. However their reaction to the same 10 per cent profit was very different. One had a positive reaction and another negative reaction. One was happy and the other unhappy. Both were affected by their reaction. However the accountant dealing with their account had neither positive of negative reaction. He was totally objective and did his job with equanimity of mind. **Happiness requires letting go of what causes suffering.**

All emotions arise in the mind (*manas*). Much of our suffering is self inflicted stimulated and provoked by mind by a lack of objectivity. A mind preoccupied with "I" and "mine" as opposed to "we" and "ours" is incapable of being objective and is doomed to suffer. A subjective mind sees the world as the source of joy and sorrow by superimposing on objects values which are not there intrinsically. Such superimposition creates likes and dislikes in our mind. Then we run towards the things we like and away from those we dislike. Our intellect (*budhihi*) is supposed to guide the mind (*manas*) to be objective. However mind is very powerful and it could overpower our intellect. Under such conditions the intellect instead of being rational begins to rationalize the conclusions of the mind to our detriment.

It is our experience that in relation to other peoples' thoughts we maintain objectivity with ease as opposed to our own thoughts. When we develop such objectivity in relation to our own thoughts we become awakened. As awakened individuals we can choose to be affected or not affected by objects and events in this world. Then thoughts cannot harm us. Certain disciplines, when scrupulously followed, can prepare our mind to be objective in dealing with our thoughts.

11

Preparation of the Mind

The actions of animals are governed exclusively by instincts. They are programmed to respond in a certain fashion to events. A donkey will kick a person pulling its tail regardless of whether the person pulling the tail is its master or a stranger. In contrast, we humans are endowed with free will. Because of our free will we have to use our discretion in choosing our actions. The choices we make will either elevate us to the level of a God or degrade us to the status of a brute.

The purpose of the disciplines we have to follow to be happy is aimed at bringing out the spiritual being, the highest personality in us. Although it is difficult to define spirituality, it is easy to recognize a spiritual person by his/her behavior. A spiritual person manifests divine qualities such as kindness, unselfishness, forgiveness, compassion, generosity, courage, and empathy when dealing with others. A spiritual person is a flower of humanity who is liked and adored by all. He has no malaise towards anyone and has good will towards all. His behavior is not governed by anticipation of reward or fear of punishment. He is what he is because he cannot be otherwise. We cannot but be impressed by such a person.

There is both diversity and unity in this world. They are like centrifugal and centripetal forces pulling in opposite directions. Diversity, which is glaringly obvious, leads to exclusiveness, and unity which is less obvious, to inclusiveness. Exclusiveness restricts and inclusiveness liberates. Our behavior is governed by our view of ourselves. For example we can view ourselves as men or women or as human beings. When we think of ourselves as men or women instead of as human beings we see diversity and become exclusive. On the contrary, when we view ourselves as human beings and not as men or women we are looking at unity and become inclusive. In our thinking we may become progressively exclusive until each one of us become isolated from everything else. If we continue to be progressively inclusive in our thinking we will reach that unity where there is only one existence. The same matter which constitutes our bodies also constitutes the sun, the moon, the stars and every other physical entity. Our physical bodies and all other physical bodies are waves in the ocean of matter. What we perceive as objects is nothing but the same matter in different forms bearing different names just as water is the content of each wave regardless of whether it is called a ripple or a breaker. The wave has no independent existence apart from the water. A wave is just a name and form depending on water for its existence. Waves come and go, but not water. The basis for everything is existence. There is only one continuous unbroken existence. A spiritual person's behavior is rooted in the vision of oneness of existence. A person who has realized this truth and in whom this truth has entered the very marrow of the person that person gains supreme happiness. To him there is no fear of death which is just a change in name and form of the body and not annihilation. When there is only one without a second how can there be fear? And who will hurt oneself? No one does. A spiritual person realizes that by hurting others he will be hurting himself. It has been well documented that when we abuse nature (integral part of existence) we hurt ourselves. A spiritual person enjoys diversity knowing that name and form, the basis for diversity, has no independent existence. Names and forms come and go just like waves having no effect on water.

A person who perceives the many as having real independent existence cannot but feel insignificantly small compared to the rest just as a wave which may feel that it is different from the ocean. Such persons cannot but feel insecure. They become fearful of the many they have to deal with. Their actions will be governed by fear, insecurity and a sense of separateness. Such a person's actions are governed by self interest at the expense of others.

Since our nature is happiness logically we should be happy all the time. But that is not the case. We are not able to realize our true nature of happiness because we cannot see ourselves in our true nature. We need a reflecting medium to reveal to us our true nature. Our situation is comparable to that of our eyes. Eyes can see everything except themselves. For the eyes to see themselves they need a reflecting medium such as a mirror. The clarity of the reflected image depends on how clean the surface of the mirror is. If the mirror is covered with dust the image will not be clear and if the covering of the dust is dense then no image will be seen at all. In addition the quality and accuracy of the reflected image depends on the surface of the mirror. If the surface is even then the reflection accurately represents the original subject without any distortion. If the surface of the mirror is uneven being convex or concave the reflection will be distorted. Our mind serves as the reflecting medium for us to view our nature. Impurities of our mind in the form of negative thoughts are like dust covering the mirror. Our inborn negative tendencies are like uneven surface of the mirror causing distortion in the reflection of our true nature. Because of these two factors we are not able to see ourselves in our true form—the source of happiness. Mind is the medium through which all knowledge takes place. To emphasize the importance of mind Krishna says in Bhagavad Gita (6:5) that mind is our best friend and also our worst enemy. This contradiction in Krishna's statement can be reconciled by understanding the scope of any equipment. No equipment is good or bad. Good or bad consequences depend on how the equipment is used. Properly managed equipment confers benefits and the improperly managed equipment causes great harm. A knife in the hands of a surgeon can save a life and the same knife in the hands of a murderer can destroy a life. Preparation of the mind is very important. Knowledge takes place only in a prepared mind. People had seen apples falling from trees from time immemorial. But it was the prepared mind of Newton that discovered the laws of gravity by observing a falling apple.

Any goal to be accomplished requires a particular life style. For example if our goal is to become an athlete then we have to spend a lot of time in the gymnasium performing physical exercise. On the other hand if our goal is to become a physician then we have to spend lot of our time with sick people studying diseases. The goal to be accomplished and the life style adopted for its accomplishment are interrelated. The goal and the means for accomplishing it are complementary and influence each another. This is true for developing an objective mind—a prerequisite for a happy life. Initially it takes conscious effort on our part to put into practice the necessary disciplines. With continued practice objectivity becomes spontaneous. **It is important to remember that it is difficult to find happiness within ourselves but it is impossible to find it anywhere else.** Therefore we should proceed with a firm resolve.

12

Transcending our Likes and Dislikes

Let us look back to our school days when we used to compete in school championship games. We liked to win and hated to lose. The game created the idea of duality of victory and defeat in us. In duality there are likes and dislikes. We were worried and agitated to gain what we liked and avoid what we disliked before and during the competition. Even if we won happiness was transient and there was agitation of losing the next game. Our life to a large extent is governed by our likes and dislikes robbing us our peace of mind. Now let us imagine that our young child has asked us to play a board game. We do not feel agitated the same way we got agitated when facing a championship game. We remain relaxed and enjoy the game regardless of victory or defeat. **Our relaxation is due to our not being under the influence of likes and dislikes but because of transcending them.** When we transcend our likes and dislikes there will be no suffering to get rid of but only happiness to enjoy.

The ultimate goal of our desires is to become happy. To fulfill our desires action is needed. **We have a choice regarding our action but not the results of the action.** For example, we have the choice of placing a porcelain plate gently on the table or throwing it on a hard floor. If we put the plate gently on the table, it will not break. If we throw it on the floor, however, it will shatter. We have the choice of placing the porcelain plate gently on the table or throwing it on the floor. We cannot perform one action and expect the result of another action. Gentle placement regardless of how often repeated will not result in a shattered plate. Nor can we throw the plate on the hard floor and expect it not to break. The result of our action is built into the action itself. With any action only four types of results are possible. They are: as expected, better than expected, less than expected, and other than expected.

Suppose you want to buy groceries. You drive to the grocery store, buy the items you need, pay the cashier, and return home. This is the type of result you would expect for the effort you have put in for going to the grocery store. Now look at another scenario. You start driving towards the grocery store but get caught in a traffic jam. When you finally reach the grocery store, the item you were seeking is not in stock. Even though you put in more effort (as compared to the previous situation), the result was less than expected. Now consider the third scenario. You go to grocery store without any hindrance. You are pleasantly surprised to find that the items you want are on sale. You save money on your purchase and feel good about it. To add to your happiness, you meet an old friend and have a pleasant conversation. In this instance, the result for the effort you put in was better than you had expected. In the last scenario, imagine that while you are driving to the grocery store, you are hit by a truck, causing you to spend several days in the hospital. For the same effort on your part, you had a result other than what you expected. How to explain the four different types of results, even though the effort put forth is the same in each of the four instances? The reason is that there are many factors which determine the outcome of any action. Our effort is only one of the variables determining the outcome of any action. Our action is processed by the laws of cosmic order and is returned to us in the form of a result. The result of any action is the net effect of the laws of cosmic order and our effort. The laws of the cosmic order are impersonal, impartial, and invariable. Therefore the result of our action under a given circumstance is always appropriate. We are neither cheated nor favored. The result of an action is built into the action itself. We have to remember that we are never deprived or deceived of what we deserved even though what we get may not be what we desired. Because of our limited knowledge and resources, we can neither foresee nor control all the variables involved to get the desired result. Therefore pragmatism dictates that we put forth the best effort and accept the result with equanimity. One may raise an objection that we can make no progress if we passively accept the results without trying to change them. Certainly, we should try to change the results. Our capacity to influence the outcome of our action is also part of the cosmic order. Change is only possible when we learn from our experience. But learning cannot and will not take place if we react with anger, disgust, depression, or frustration when we encounter failure. Only a calm, undistracted, vigorous mind can analyze the cause of failure or success and learn from it. Take the example of Sir Alexander Fleming. He was trying to culture some bacteria in his laboratory. On one occasion the bacteria had not grown the way he had expected. With an objective mind he analyzed and investigated the failure to grow bacteria. His studies lead to the discovery of penicillin—a great boom for humanity to fight infection. If he had become angry, disgusted or overcome with sense of self pity at his failure to grow the bacteria and discarded the containers in which he was trying to culture the bacteria he would have missed the opportunity of discovering penicillin. He succeeded because he had the equanimity of mind which enabled him to look objectively at the result of his action (growing bacteria).

The purpose of rituals is to make abstract principles concrete. Our ancestors have bequeathed us a beautiful ritual to make the abstract principle that we have a choice in our action but not on their results and we should not get lured by inaction. Hindus when they visit a temple for worshiping God, they take an offering (*naivedyam*) to God (cosmic order). The offering may be a fruit, flower, leaves or some food item. Regardless of the choice of the offering, the best possible item in that category is selected for the offering. The selection process is symbolic of the best effort we should put into our actions. Different devotees offer different items to God. After the worship, the offerings made is distributed to the devotees by the priest. There is no guarantee that the devotees will receive the same item they had offered. They will get one item from the collection of offerings made which may not be what they offered. What comes from the altar is called *prasadam* and it may consist of water, fruit, flower or something edible etc. Regardless of whatever is received as *prasadam* it is accepted gracefully without resistance and with equanimity. The ritual is designed to reinforce the idea that we should put our best effort when performing an action and accept the results of the action with grace and equanimity. This is the secret to transcend our likes and dislikes— a necessary requisite for our happiness.

13

Pain and Suffering

When President Lincoln was about to deliver his presidential inaugural address a rich aristocrat stood up and said, "Mr. Lincoln, you should not forget that your father used to make shoes for my family." The whole senate laughed thinking that the man had made a fool of Lincoln. The man intended, probably consumed by his own jealousy at Lincoln's achievement, to hurt him and make him unhappy on one of the most memorable days of his life. Unfortunately there are many people in this world who gain pleasure by hurting others. We cannot escape such incidences. But the truth is that no one can hurt us unless we allow them to hurt us. Lincoln illustrated this truth from his spontaneous response to that "gentleman's" remark. Most of us, if we were in Lincoln's position, would have been deeply hurt and expressed our hurt feeling. But Lincoln was made of a different stuff. He directly looked at the man in the eyes and said, "Sir, I know that my father used to make shoes for your family and many others here. He made shoes the way nobody else can. He was a creator. His shoes were not just shoes. He poured his whole soul into them. I want to ask you 'Have you any complaints?' I know how to make shoes myself. If you have any complaints I can make you another pair of shoes. But as far as I know nobody has ever complained about my father's shoes. He was a genius and a great creator. I am proud of my father." The whole senate was struck dumb. Lincoln rose in their esteem by demonstrating an intelligent way of handling a painful incident to avoid getting hurt. Lincoln exercised his option not to suffer from the pain inflicted on him.

In this world there are plenty of problems which can cause us pain. But suffering is optional. Our response to a painful condition determines whether we get crushed or come out more brilliant like a polished diamond as Lincoln did. For not being crushed by a painful situation we should clearly understand the difference between pain and suffering. Sometimes the words pain and suffering are used as synonyms. Here for our discussion they will be considered as two separate words with different meanings. Pain is a physiologic process. It is a signal of injury to a part of the body including mind. The information concerning injury is transmitted to the brain as electrical impulses through nerve fibers. Once the brain receives the information it can take further action not only to prevent continued exposure to the injurious agent but also to mobilize forces for healing. Therefore pain plays an important role in self preservation. Pain is physical. Suffering is mental. Suffering is our reaction to the perception of pain. In other words suffering is subjective. Pain means different things to different people. While pain cannot be modified the experience of suffering can be modified for better or for worse depending on whether it is considered avoidable or unavoidable, useful or useless, and deserved or undeserved.

If someone is pricked with a needle intentionally with malice that person's reaction will be different compared to that of an accidental prick. In the former instance the incidence will be perceived as avoidable and undeserved. The suffering experienced will be greater and the response will tend to be more violent compared to that of an accidental prick. Suppose the same person decides to have tattooing of his body, or body piercing to wear an ornament. No doubt brain receives nerve impulses of injury to the body which will be interpreted as pain. However little or no suffering is experienced since reaction to pain is modified. In this situation pain is welcomed. Although the person doing the tattoo or body piercing has caused pain that person is thanked. Suffering is an emotion resulting from pain perceived as unjust accompanied by a sense of victimization.

Little or no suffering is experienced if the pain is associated with a secondary gain. It is well known that soldiers who get shot and are removed from the front line require lot less narcotics to control their pain compared to civilians with comparable injuries. The difference in response is due to how the injury and its associated pain is perceived. For a soldier pain of injury is associated with a secondary gain. The soldier welcomes the pain as it enables him to be moved to a relatively safe hospital bed compared to the dangers in the front line. On the contrary for a civilian the pain is not welcome as it requires him to move to a hospital bed which is less comfortable than his domestic set up. For the civilian there is no secondary gain. For the civilian the pain is an intruder disrupting normal daily activity. Therefore for the civilian pain is unwelcome and he suffers more compared to the soldier.

Every religion recommends austerities for one's spiritual growth. Austerities involve certain amount of pain. However austerities are gladly undertaken by the faithful without any sense of suffering. Similarly at a secular level athletes for outperforming others or themselves undergo painful practices but do not consider it suffering. The conclusion we can draw from the above observations is that suffering can be defanged by welcoming pain.

We will be able to welcome pain if we understand that both pleasant and unpleasant experiences are for our growth and development. As a matter of fact unpleasant experiences, if accepted with a proper attitude, prove to be more potent compared to pleasant experiences in promoting our growth and development. Unpleasant experiences should be viewed as millions of hits from chisel and hammer a stone has to endure to become a beautiful statue.

14

Nonviolence (*ahimsa*)

ahimsa means not injuring any living being with words, thought, and deeds. No living creature likes to be hurt or killed. As individuals we do not want others to hurt us. What we do not want others do to us, we should not do to others. This natural instinctive expectation is the basis for the practice of *ahimsa* which is a universal law. When a universal law is transgressed nothing happens to the law but the transgressor suffers.

We live in society and have to interact with other members of the society. It is natural to have some expectations from other members of the society. When our expectations are not met it is natural to become impulsive and hurt the responsible person. An action based on impulsive behavior will result in future guilt and regrets. Only a sensitive mind which can feel the hurt of others can stop this instinctive and impulsive behavior. When we get hurt by someone else's words or deeds we may not be able to retaliate immediately under the prevailing circumstances and will wait for the right moment to settle the score. In that situation we may end up carrying the violent impulse in our heart for a long time committing violence against ourselves and will remain unhappy. As long as we harbor such feelings practice of *ahimsa* is impossible. *ahimsa* includes not hurting ourselves. *ahimsa* should begin with oneself.

ahimsa is only the first step. Continued practice of *ahimsa* will culminate in universal love. Love is being good to others without expecting anything in return and not stopping even if the recipient of our love were to hurt us. Love, one of the most frequently used word, is also the most misunderstood. It is often confused with attachment. Love and attachment are distinctly different. Love is liberating and attachment is binding. Attachment is conditional and love is unconditional. In attachment the concern is what one gets and in love the emphasis is on what one can give. What one gets is not ignored but it is secondary to what one gives. There is bondage in attachment and freedom in love. Attachment is born out of weakness and love out of strength. In love we allow others to depend on us and it is a sign of strength. In attachment we depend on others for our happiness and it is a sign of weakness. Attachment leads to sorrow. The problem of attachment is universal even though the object of attachment varies from person to person and for the same person from time to time. Attachment leads to intellectual clouding culminating in violation of moral and ethical principles.

Even when we are not able to help others in their distress physically we can send compassionate thoughts towards them and comfort them with words. We should never underestimate the importance of individual thoughts. Human history is nothing but an account of the thoughts of single individuals influencing the collective consciousness for better or worse. So we should never lose the opportunity for sending out compassionate thoughts towards others especially for those in distress. Any good action we do will be processed by the laws of creation and will be returned to us as happiness. The return may be immediate or delayed but the result is inescapable just as day follows night.

15

Accommodation (*ksantihi*) and Forgiveness (*kshamA*)

Both accommodation and forgiveness are closely related. One cannot be practiced without the other. Accommodation refers to acceptance of choice-less situations in life without bitterness, self pity, frustration, and anger towards oneself, world or God. Such an attitude conserves our energy and allows it to be diverted for constructive work. Past is a choice-less situation. So too is the present which has taken birth from the womb of the past. There is only the possibility of changing our future. Any change requires time. That means patience has to be developed. Acceptance of these facts frees one from stress. Only a stressed person commits violence (*himsa*) on himself and on others.

To develop accommodation we should give up our demand that another person or situation should change for the sake of our happiness. Understanding the nature of people will help in developing accommodation. No one person will either have all the qualities we like or dislike. We are all a mixture of desirable and not so desirable qualities. So no one will find us unreservedly likable. Just as we expect others to change for our convenience they in turn want us to change for their convenience creating a no win situation at its best or a conflict at its worst. Since we are not willing or able to change to meet others' expectations, we should be charitable enough to let others be what they are. Allowing others to be what they are is accommodation. **All relationships require accommodation. Accommodation is the best antidote against unfairly judging people.**

Paradoxically we will be more accommodative to strangers than to our own near and dear ones. This is because we do not expect anything from strangers but a lot from those close to us. When a stranger does something not in conformity with our expectations our reaction may be one of indifference, surprise or amusement. But when the actions of our near and dear ones are not in conformity with our expectations we feel disappointed or angry.

To be happy we should accept people as they are in the same way as we accept inert objects. We do not expect inert objects to be different from what they are. We do not expect fire to become cold in summer for our comfort. We accept fire as it is. We are objective in our acceptance.

When a person's actions are not to our liking we become unhappy. So long as we remain focused on the action it is hard to be accommodative. To be accommodative we should understand the person behind the act. The response of a person to a given incidence is governed by that person's background. If we view someone's action as a product of that person's background then we realize that the outcome could not have been any different. The outcome would be viewed as the most appropriate response under the given circumstance. May be, if we had the same background of that person, our response would not have been any different. When we cultivate such a frame of mind we will be freeing ourselves from the habit of mechanical response to actions of others. We will remain objective. We become accommodative.

Some of our own weaknesses and actions may be unacceptable to us. So there is a need not only to accommodate others but also ourselves. Accommodation does not mean acceptance what is wrong. It is accepting the person as he is without necessarily approving the action. If a child dirties a nice dress the mother will not approve of the action of the child but does not disown the child. She cleans the child and does her best to help the child to remain clean. Accommodation and forgiveness has to be practiced in that spirit. We should develop compassion for others' weakness but never justify our own. We should strive to overcome our weaknesses. When we are not accommodative we develop deep aversion. As prisoners of aversion resulting from our own or others' actions we cannot live our lives fully. We will be tormented from the burden of guilt and anger. We need to free ourselves from this prison and it is only possible by forgiveness. There are three parts to forgiveness. 1. Seeking forgiveness from those whom we have harmed. 2. Offering forgiveness to those who have harmed us. 3. Forgiving oneself for acts of omissions and commissions coupled with a resolve of not repeating them.

Forgiveness is a powerful value worth cultivation. The aversion we feel for others or for ourselves when we fail to be accommodative may turn into hatred and thoughts of revenge. Violence which accompanies hatred and vengeance is not conquered by hate but by love and forgiveness. This principle was emphasized by Buddha 2500 years ago, to his disciples, by narrating the story of Dirgayu which is recorded in Maha Vagga.

Brahmadatta was a powerful king of Kashi. He wanted to enlarge his kingdom and attacked Kosala a smaller weaker neighboring kingdom.

Dirgheti, the king of Kosala, knew that his army was no match to that of the powerful Brahmadatta. To avoid futile bloodshed he abandoned his kingdom and lived incognito with his wife. While he was living incognito a son was born to him. He named his son Dirgayu. Dirgheti knew that Brahmadatta was in pursuit of him and his family. Fearing for the life of Dirgayu, Dirgheti sent Dirgayu away and arranged for his education. When Dirgayu returned after finishing his education, he found that his parents had been captured by Brahmadatta and were being taken for execution. Dirgheti saw Dirgayu in the crowd. He wanted to give him a message but without exposing his identity. So he said aloud, "Hatred is not appeased by hatred; hatred is only appeased by nonhatred." Dirgheti and his wife were executed.

Dirgayu procured employment in Brahmadatta's court. He became a favorite of Brahmadatta by his exemplary service. One day Brahmadatta went on a hunting expedition. It so happened that Brahmadatta and Dirgayu got separated from the rest of the retinue. Exhausted, Brahmadatta fell asleep under the shade of a tree. Dirgayu felt that the time to avenge the death of his parents was ripe. He was about to draw his sword to kill Brahmadatta. But he remembered his father's last words that hatred is not appeased by hatred. He gave up the idea of killing Brahmadatta even though he had a chance. At about the same time Brahmadatta awoke perspiring and with fright. Dirgayu asked Brahmadatta the cause of his fright. He replied, "My sleep is always disturbed. I often dream of the son of Dirgheti coming towards me with a sword to kill me and avenge the death of his parents." Dirgayu then said, "I am the son of Dirgheti. I was about to kill you. But I remembered my father's words. If I had killed you, your people would have tried to avenge your death by killing me. The cycle of avenging would have continued. To prevent such an unfortunate situation from developing

I have forgiven you remembering my father's last words. I do not want to kill you. You may rest without fear." Brahmadatta was moved by Dirgayu's thoughts and action. He felt repentant for what he had done to Dirgheti and his wife. Overcome with repentance for his past action, Brahmadatta gave his daughter in marriage to Dirgayu and made him the king of Kosala.

This story illustrates that the both Brahmadatta and Dirgayu were suffering and unhappy until they broke the vicious cycle of hatred and anger by forgiving each other. In this world everything is undergoing constant change under the influence of time. It is worth remembering that an unpleasant incident too is transient and the incident becomes a thing of the past. The one to forgive and the one to be forgiven also change. They do not remain the same persons as they were when the undesirable event happened. Therefore opportunities should not be lost to build bridges to start relationships afresh.

We cannot dismiss the above narration of Buddha as fiction with little relevance in real life. The narration has great relevance. Such events do happen in this world. Approximately 300 years after the death of Buddha, Emperor Asoka waged a brutal war against Kalingas for expanding his kingdom. He was moved by the misery he had caused for the Kalingas. He was repelled by his own action and unacceptable to himself. He realized that the price for expanding his kingdom was unacceptably high. To become acceptable to himself he decided to renounce violence. He came to the conclusion that the only victory worth having is that won by changing the heart of his opponents. He successfully implemented this concept into practice during his subsequent long peaceful reign.

More recently Mahatma Gandhi pointed out the havoc of hatred and vengeance when he said that an eye for an eye will make the whole world blind. He did not choose the path of violence against the British who had colonized India. Instead he followed the path of *ahimsa* and accommodation to liberate India from colonial bondage. Another example is that of Martin Luther King Jr. who followed the path of Mahatma Gandhi to eliminate racial inequality in the U.S.A.

16

Integrity

A group of musicians casually coming together do not constitute an orchestra. They constitute an orchestra only when they work in unison with their musical instruments. Only then there will be delightful music. For us to be happy our thoughts, words and actions should be in unison just as musicians are in an orchestra. When there is nonalignment of our thoughts, actions and words we develop a split personality. A gulf will be created between the thinking person, talking person and the doing person. The resultant gulf creates a restless mind troubled by guilt and conflict. Such a mind is an unhappy mind. Persons with a split personality will have difficulty communicating with themselves and with others. Self conceit is a threat for integration of our thoughts, words, and actions. We have to be free from self conceit which makes its appearance in two forms. Two Sanskrit words are used to denote absence of these two forms of self conceit. They are *amAnitvam* and *adhambithvam*. They have some similarities as well as differences.

Absence of Self Adoration (*amAnitvam*)

The word *amAnitvam* has its origin in the Sanskrit word *mAna* which means exaggerated sense of self adoration. The word does not refer to positive self image one should have about oneself. Self respect is healthy and is desirable. *mAnitvam* is a state of mind requiring adoration from others for whatever qualification the person may possess. The sense of self adoration is not expressed outwardly but is psychologically felt. It is the duty of a society to admire, recognize and reward the accomplishments of its members. But if one joins the society in self adoration it becomes problematic. The problem for a *mani* (one who has sense of self adoration) is that he considers that what he has is more important than what he is. He attaches disproportionate significance to whatever he has in terms of possessions or accomplishments. He expects others to adore him for his possessions or accomplishments. *amAnitvam* means to be free from self adoration.

A clear understanding of the basis for adoration will be of great help in freeing ourselves from the grip of self adoration. The basis for adoration varies. If we possess something for which someone has a value we will be adored on the basis of our possession. If we are looked upon as rich, people who cherish money will adore us. It is important to recognize that the adoration is essentially for money and not so much for us. If we were to lose our money we will no longer be adored. We live in an ephemeral world. It is a rule rather than an exception for our positions and possessions to keep on changing. We are painfully aware that presidents become past presidents, professionals become retirees, and fortunes are made and lost.

A second reason for adoration is the fancy of individuals. Someone who has a fancy for some of our possession or position may adore us. The fancy of individuals also keeps changing. When the individual loses fancy for what we possess we will cease to be an object of adoration. In addition one *mAni* will not be able to adore another *mAni* because of his own psychological requirements. A *mAni* thinks he is the best in his field of activity. Therefore expects adoration from the rest. Sooner or later someone better comes along and *mAni's* bloated ego gets deflated. When we start believing that we deserve adoration from others that feeling wets our appetite for more and more adoration. We develop addiction for adoration. When we are no longer adored we suffer just as a drug addict suffers from withdrawal from drugs.

The reason a *mAni* needs adoration from others is because of his own doubt about his qualifications for adoration. The demand for adoration on others is due to *mAni's* need to be assured that he is somebody. This inner urge is due to his inability to accept his own limitations. He is unacceptable to himself.

Absence of Pretence (*adhambhitvam*)

adhambitvam means absence of *dhambitvam*. *dhamba* means pretence. Self adoration is common to both *mAnitvam* and *dhambitvam*. However the basis for self adoration is different. The conceit of a *mAni* is based on his own achievement whereas that of a *dhambi* (one who has dhambha) on achievements that are not his. He expects adoration because of achievements of his family members or friends. He tries to impress others by claiming acquaintance with people with name and fame in high places when in fact he may not even be familiar to his local city councilor. He has no achievements of his own deserving adoration. For adoration he resorts to pretension. For example a *dhambi* to impress others may pretend to be a rich man wearing borrowed costly designer clothes when in fact he has very little bank balance. Such a person should be always on his guard and have a good memory to avoid being exposed. How can such a person be happy?

mAnitvam and *dambhitvam* are the outcome of not understanding the nature of any accomplishment. They drop off automatically when one critically analyses the nature of any accomplishment. A *mAni* demands adoration because of his fallacious thinking that he is totally responsible for his accomplishments. The fallacy of his thinking is easy to expose. For any accomplishment one needs a physical body as a first prerequisite. We are not the creators of our own physical body. It was given to us. It came with certain inherent potentials. What one can do is to exploit its potentials. Furthermore even in exploitation of one's potentials the sheer ability is not a determinant of success. Any achievement is possible only when opportunities are provided. And the entire world is responsible for providing any opportunity. This concept can be best understood by means of an example. Let us suppose a surgeon performs a successful operation. Can he claim exclusive credit for the success of the operation? The answer is no. A surgeon can claim only a small role for the successful operation. His performance was based on the contribution of innumerable number of factors and people. Among the many factors responsible for the success of the operation let us start our discussion with one simple item like the surgical knife which is often taken for granted. The steel from which the knife is manufactured had to be mined. Mining involves the effort of a lot of people. The mined ore had to be transformed to steel which again involves a large number of people. The steel then required to be transformed to knife which again is the result of effort of a large number of people. The manufactured knife needed transportation to the site of operation requiring the effort of more people. The technology of mining, manufacturing and transportation has developed over centuries and in each century people have contributed to technological advances of the present day knife. Not only people were involved in technological advances but also in transmitting that knowledge for future generations which required teachers and their support systems. What applies to one item applies to every item the surgeon used in executing the operation including the help of the team assisting the surgeon. If we keep analyzing in this fashion we cannot but conclude that the whole humanity, both past and present, has directly or indirectly contributed to the success of the operation. Furthermore animal kingdom too can claim a share in the success of the operation based on its contribution as experimental animals for the advancement of medical knowledge. The contribution of plant kingdom is even greater. Plant kingdom has sustained whole of the animal kingdom by providing food in addition to medicines for the success of the operation. By a thoughtful consideration of any accomplishment one cannot escape the realization that the whole creation is one interdependent and interconnected organic whole of which we are an integral inseparable part. Nothing happens in isolation. With that realization *mAnitvam* drops by itself. What is then left is *amAnitvam* and such a person will no longer be dependent on others adoration for his happiness. He will be happy and acceptable to himself for having played his part.

17

Absence of Sense of Ownership (*asaktihi*)

The word *sakti means* clinging attachment to things based on the notion of ownership. *asakti* refers to the attitude of absence of notion of ownership. It is an attitude that we do not owe anything. **Ownership is notional whereas possession is factual.**

This world we live in is a like a guest house. There are many wonderful things provided in this guest house for us to use and be happy. Many people before us have used the facilities and many more will use in the future. So we cannot claim ownership but only temporary possession. The attitude of not owning anything will have significant implications for our happiness and it will become evident from the following example. Suppose we are living in a rented house. Any repairs that need to be attended will be the responsibility of the owner of the house. We will not be burdened with the responsibility of the maintenance of the house in terms of repair, paying taxes, insurance etc. If we happen to purchase the same house we become the owners and incur all the responsibilities. Instead of enjoying our stay in the house we will be worried about its maintenance. Even a little deterioration of the paint will be a sufficient cause to rob our peace of mind and make us unhappy.

Our attitude of not owning should not be limited to material objects. It should include our near and dear ones. We have our duties towards them but we should not get excessively attached to them. Excessive attachment is when we feel all is lost and life is not worth living when we are separated from a near and dear one for whatever reason (estrangement, demand of jobs, and death etc). We all came to this world alone accompanied by none and will be leaving this world alone without anyone joining us. Separation from our dear and near ones sooner or later is a fact of life in this ephemeral world of ours.

We are born as human beings. We become a husband or a wife after marriage. Husband or wife is a role we acquire. No one is born as a husband or a wife. During our life span we pick up various roles. If a spouse were to die, from the list of our roles, one role—husband or wife role—drops out. But the rest of the roles continue. Our identity is not confined to any one relationship. But what happens is that when the role we consider important ceases, it adversely affects our entire personality. One may become pathologically depressed and may even commit suicide.

Absence of excessive attachment is not a recipe for negligence in the performance of our duties. We have duties to our family members, friends, employers, employees and for many others. These duties have to be meticulously discharged. Absence of excessive attachment is viewing things objectively and having the right perspective. A person endowed with this attribute will not avoid relationships but understands their fragility. Being aware of the fragility that person will make the best use of all relationships. Such a person functions like a tourist. Suppose someone is visiting America as a tourist with limited duration of stay. Being acutely aware of the limited time as a tourist, that person wastes no time and sees as many tourist attractions as possible. A tourist will in all probability see more places than many American citizens. Americans living in America are in no hurry to visit places in their own country since they think that they have plenty of time and can visit those places at anytime they desire. They take for granted that they will be there forever, but die without seeing those places. Therefore, like a tourist, a person without excessive attachment enjoys all relationships. The relationships do not become a source of sorrow; they become a recipe for celebration of life.

18

Happiness through Work

According to Thomas Aquinas there can be no joy of life without joy of work. We derive happiness when our work makes a genuine contribution to ourselves and to our fellow human beings. With the advent of industrial revolution work places have progressively become larger and impersonal. They have become too big to be incomprehensible to know who is served by our work and to what extent. Work seems to lack meaningful involvement. Work for many of us has become a drudgery. To allow work, which occupies a major portion of our waking hours, to be a source of unhappiness is indeed a tragedy. It is essential that we convert our work from being a drudgery to a fulfilling experience. Can it be done?

A number of stone masons were working chiseling stones. A visitor asked several of them the same question, namely, "What are you doing?" He got different replies from each of them.

One mason said, "Are you blind? Can you not see what I am doing?"

Another replied, "I am chiseling a stone."

The third one said, "I am earning a livelihood to support my family."

The fourth one said, "I am building a temple for people to worship God and get peace of mind."

Although the four masons were engaged in the same type of work and were paid the same amount of wages for their work the happiness they derived from their work was vastly different. The first mason represents those who see no worth in their work and hence angry with themselves and the world. They are most unhappy. The second mason represents those who pass their time working passively in a mechanical fashion. They are like robots. They are a little better than the first group in that they are at least not angry with themselves and with the world. The third mason represents those who have an aim but that aim is to benefit a limited circle of their kith and kin. They are happy to a limited extent so long as they are able to satisfy the material needs of their near and dear ones. The fourth mason represents those who have a large heart and work for the benefit of humanity. They see themselves as useful and contributing citizens. They have converted their work as a source of happiness. They are happy people. The example illustrates that by a change in our orientation we can convert our work from one of drudgery to one of fulfillment. **To be happy is our choice.**

The next question is how to bring about a change in our attitude. While discussing *amAnitvam* it was pointed out that we are a part and parcel of the whole universe which is an interconnected interdependent organic whole. In an interconnected and interdependent system every entity has a role to play and intern is affected by everything else for better or for worse. When we were born we were totally helpless and would have perished if we had not received help from many sources. As we grew older our dependence gradually became less and less. The help we received is a form of debt. As debtors we have a duty to pay back our debt. The time to repay the debt is when we grow older and become productive citizens of the society. We grew up as receivers which created in us a tendency to grab and not to give. We have to understand that there is a time to receive and there is a time to give. We cannot be receivers all the time. To be receivers all the time is against the law of creation. We may adhere to the law and pay back our debt willingly and be happy knowing that we are becoming free from our debt. On the other hand when we are derelicts in our duty of paying back the debt it will be extracted by us forcibly. Forcible extraction causes pain in the form of unhappiness.

When we abide by the laws of creation we will be happy. It will be like sailing in the direction of the wind. The whole creation is based on the concept of receiving and giving. For example rivers empty their water into the ocean. The ocean which receives water from the rivers sends it back to them through clouds in the form of rain. Hoarding in any form which obstructs the smooth flow of give and take is against the law of creation. There is a penalty to be paid for transgressing the law of creation in the form of unhappiness. The law of creation demands that we should give to be happy. It has been well documented that those who render voluntary service in helping others are more satisfied with their life. They are more peaceful and happy, and less prone to depression. Giving is surprisingly a potent force in nourishing health and happiness in astonishing ways based on recent medical research.

It has been previously pointed out that we are part of the universe which is one interconnected, interrelated, organic whole. The corollary is that we will be subject to the effects of our own actions we undertake—good or bad. If we were to burn a part of our body like the arm we suffer. If he help our arm from getting burnt we will be helping ourselves. In a like fashion we will be hurting ourselves when we hurt others and will be helping ourselves when we help others. Therefore we should indulge in good actions and avoid bad actions. What, then, is the criterion for determining whether an action is good or bad? The determining factor is the intent behind the action. An action undertaken with a good intent will produce virtue (*punya*) and an action undertaken with bad intent will produce sin (*papa*). A good action is an appropriate action under a given situation; a bad action is an inappropriate action for a given situation. The golden rule for determining the appropriateness of an action is indeed simple. Confucius said that the central principle of appropriate action is not to do anything that you would not have done to you. Hindu scriptures proclaim that non-injury (*ahimsa*) is the highest duty. Tzu-Kung asked his master for one word that could serve as a rule of practice for all life. The master replied, "Is not reciprocity such a word? What you do not want done to yourself, do not do to others." The Bible tells us, "All things whatsoever you would that men should do to you, do you even so to them."

Performing work with the spirit of helping others is to be in harmony with oneself. "Goodness" Thoreau wrote, "Is the only investment that never fails." Being good to others is like prepaying a debt. Happiness we gain by helping others is comparable to the interest we save by prepaying our debt. The total interest to be paid becomes less. The money so saved becomes available to us to be used at our discretion for other purposes. Opportunities for us to be kind to others by our words, thoughts and deeds are indeed numerous and the opportunity should never be lost.

According to cosmology it is estimated that our universe is approximately 15 billion years old. It is supposed to have originated with the "big bang". After the big bang the whole creation proceeded in a hierarchical fashion—the formation of small simple structures preceding and then contributing to the formation of larger complex ones. In the beginning the universe was incredibly hot. It was too hot for even subatomic particles to exist. In approximately 300,000 years the universe became sufficiently cool when the simplest Hydrogen and Helium atoms could come into existence. It took many billions of years for large scale structures such as earliest stars, galaxies and super clusters to come into existence. It is estimated that in about a billion years the distance between the sun and earth decreases due to expansion of the sun. Because of the Sun becoming closer to earth, the earth becomes too hot to support life. Life on earth becomes extinct. In approximately 5 billion years the earth itself ceases to exist by being engulfed by the expanding Sun.

It took approximately 10 billion years of physical evolution for our earth to come into existence. Simple life forms appeared on earth about four billion years ago. The biological evolution, for a long time, then proceeded at a slow pace. It took another three billion years for complex multicellular organisms to evolve. The earliest mammals made their appearance about 250 million years ago; humans only 45 thousand years ago. In evolutionary time scale humans are on this earth for a very brief period of time. We are the product of a long evolutionary process governed by laws of creation. These laws existed long before we came on the scene and will continue even if human species were to vanish from the surface of the earth. We are not the creators of the laws but are subject to these laws. Wisdom consists in adapting to the laws which cannot be changed. But we expect the laws to change to suit our fancy, which does not happen, leaving us frustrated and unhappy.

From the narrow perspective of our tiny life span it is hard to comprehend that there is a plan and purpose for creation and for human existence. We have to realize that as we travel through our own lives we also travel through the life of our universe which has a life of its own with a beginning, an end and a period of existence in between. In other words our life is closely intertwined with the life of the universe we live in. It is too simplistic to attribute our presence in this universe to chance, which explains nothing. It has taken billions of years of creation to prepare a place like earth for us to inhabit. Earth is the only planet where live forms exist in our solar system. Viewed from the broader perspective taking into consideration the progression of creation and the unique place we occupy in it in terms of space and time, it is not inconceivable that there is a plan and purpose for the creation. It appears that creation has its own plan and we are part of the plan even though we are not able to comprehend it with our limitations. Each one of us is a special entity serving the purpose and plan of the creation in a unique way. In the plan and purpose of the creation we are all indispensable. We have our assigned place and role. From the perspective of totality no role is superior or inferior but appropriate to our level of evolution. What is required of us is to efficiently and willingly play the assigned role. If we work with such an understanding work will be a fulfilling experience and we will be happy.

19

God and Happiness

We, human beings, are intrigued regarding the origin and purpose of the universe and our role in it. We have been searching for answers from time immemorial. Even at the very early stages of development human beings must have experienced the beneficial as well as the harmful effects of powerful natural forces such as wind, fire, and water on their life. For example they must have happily experienced the warmth of fire in winter and greatly distressed when their meager possessions were consumed by it. They must have viewed the forces of nature which could be both benevolent and malevolent with a complex sense of awe, fear, respect, love, and hatred. Regardless of their attitude towards these elements, they had to deal with them. For dealing with the elements they adopted two approaches.

With the passage of time humans understood that there was an order in the functioning of the powerful natural forces and planetary bodies like the sun and the moon. They observed that every day the sun rose in the east and set in the west. The moon waxed and waned in a regular fashion. They noticed that everything functioned in a systematic and compliant manner. Each powerful force functioned within its own limitations and never transgressed it. For instance, water flowed from a higher level to a lower level but never from a lower to a higher level. Fire always made objects close to it hot and not cold. It appeared as though the elements were obediently serving a higher more powerful entity. This higher powerful entity was given the name God. The occurrence of natural disasters brought on by elements was viewed as wrath of God as punishment for the sins of omissions and commissions of human beings. It was reasoned that to prevent natural calamities responsible for human misery, God had to be propitiated. Propitiation took the form of rituals. Priest craft and religion was the outcome of the need to develop and perform rituals on a regular basis.

Side by side with the development of religion and priest craft, observation and experimentation with the natural forces continued. From these observations and experiments it was learnt that the power in the elements could be harnessed for human good. This second approach resulted in the development of science. The basis for religion was faith; for science the basis was reason.

Religion and science based on faith and reason respectively superficially appear to be opposed to each other but indeed they are complimentary. In religion the emphasis is on moral, ethical and spiritual laws governing the creation. The emphasis in science is on physical, chemical, and biological laws governing the creation. Science and religion cater to the needs of different components of our personality. Science based on reasoning appeals to our intellect. Science, which empowers us to control our external environment, has contributed to our physical comfort. However our happiness is governed to a great extent by emotions. Much attention has been given in our educational systems for physical and intellectual development but unfortunately not enough for emotional development. Therefore it is not uncommon for even the so called successful people to be miserable failures in their personal life because of their inability to handle emotional relationships. Emotions have great power. Like any power it may prove constructive or destructive depending on how it is handled. The power of emotions has to be harnessed for our advantage. The type of emotions we develop depends on how we perceive and react to events we are faced with. For example when someone criticizes us we may take it as an insult or as an opportunity for introspection and for our improvement. The choice is ours. If we feel insulted we become angry and may hurt ourselves and also the one who insulted us. On the other hand if we accept it as an opportunity for our improvement we will be thankful and there is a good chance we improve ourselves. **Our attitude makes the difference.** Let us consider another example. Faced with others' success we may become jealous. But with success of our own children we become happy. The reason for the differences in response is that we see ourselves in our children. When we see ourselves in the other person love comes naturally. Where there is love there will be no place for negative destructive emotions like anger, hatred, jealousy, or violence. Religion aims at making us more loving. For this purpose religion advances the concept of existence of a loving God as a role model for us to follow.

In our solar system earth is unique in having living creatures. Why is life absent from other planets? This observation is explained by cosmologists on the basis of anthropic principle. The principle recognizes that there are properties of the universe that are necessary for the evolution and persistence of life within it. Many factors need to come together within a particular range for life forms to become a possibility. The universe began with the big bang and the universe started expanding at a tremendous rate. If the rate of expansion was faster than what it was, the material would have dispersed farther apart preventing formation of galaxies and stars. On the other hand if the expansion was slower, then the material would have coalesced into dense masses causing a universe of black holes instead of hydrogen burning stars like our sun capable of producing light and heat required for sustaining life. The rate of expansion was just right for galaxies and planets to form.

There is another link between the expanding universe and life forms. Chemical elements like carbon, oxygen, silicone etc. are necessary to produce complex chemical substances on which life depends. These elements were not present in the universe when it first appeared. These elements came into existence in the stars over billions of years through a sequence of nuclear reactions by a combination of two helium nuclei resulting in the formation the element beryllium. By addition of another helium nucleus to beryllium carbon came into existence. Further addition of another helium nucleus to carbon resulted in the formation of oxygen and the process continued to produce all the other elements of the periodic table. The process took place in the dying stars under suitable temperature for the reactions to occur. When a dying star exploded in a supernova then the elements were dispersed in the universe as space dust and the condensed dust gave rise to formation of new planets containing these elements. Ultimately these elements contributed to the formation of the body of living organisms like us.

It is evident from our knowledge of cosmology that there is a close connection between large scale properties of the universe and the existence of life within it. For example there are many factors responsible for life forms to originate and evolve on earth. Let us consider the size of earth. The size is optimal to have gravity sufficient to hold the atmosphere extending over 50 miles above the surface of the earth. If the earth were smaller its gravitational power would have been weak to hold the atmosphere, a necessary requisite for life forms to appear. On the contrary if the earth was more massive in size, its atmosphere would be like that of Jupiter which consists of only hydrogen. Earth is the only planet in our solar system equipped with an atmosphere of right mixture of gases to sustain life as we know it.

The distance of earth from the sun is also an important factor. If the earth was a little farther from the sun it would have been frozen and if it was little closer it would have been too hot to sustain life. In addition the earth rotates on its own axis once every 24 hours allowing the entire surface of the earth to be properly warmed and cooled every day. The position of earth in relation to the sun makes available plenty of water without which living organisms cannot survive. Water which many of us take for granted has many wonderful properties. The variation between its boiling and freezing point allows living creatures live in an environment of fluctuating temperatures. Water being a universal solvent can carry chemicals, nutrients and minerals throughout the body of living organisms. Being chemically neutral it can carry these substances without affecting their properties.

An observation is open to be interpreted differently by different people based on their background. The cosmological observations which explain the appearance and existence of life on earth are interpreted differently by science and religion. The former explains it on the basis of chance. According to religion that too many things had to come together to create a suitable environment for emergence of life and cannot be attributed to chance. According to religion a life giving factor is responsible for fine tuning the events underlying the machinery and design of the universe. The principle or the entity responsible for fine tuning the events following the big bang is given the name God. Both science and religion recognize that the universe, which includes us, is governed by laws. For science all the laws are impersonal and for religion they are personified in God. However both are in agreement that the laws governing the creation have to be observed for us to be happy.

We are all born with ignorance of ourselves and of the world. When we are born we do not even know that there are manmade laws which we have to follow for harmoniously living in a society. We grow up observing the dos and don'ts as prescribed by authoritative figures like our parents, teachers and others motivated either by fear or love. When we followed the dos and don'ts of authoritative figures we were following different laws even without knowing the existence of the laws. The habit of following the dos and don'ts of authoritative figures has been ingrained in us from an early age. For prompting us to adhere to laws of creation religion presents God as the ultimate authoritative figure and scriptures as the repository of God's dos and don'ts.

Majority of human beings pray to God either regularly or on occasion. Prayer is a voluntary action. Since prayer is a voluntary activity one may or may not do it. Then why do the majority of people pray and is there any rationale? Every action produces a result. The result may be immediate or delayed. When it is delayed it is difficult to understand the cause and effect relationship between the action and its result. Since prayer is an action it too should produce some result. We pray for the fulfillment of our desires. All our desires in the ultimate analysis are for making us happy. We become disappointed when prayer does not immediately produce the desired result. We forget that the results of prayer are not always immediate but may be delayed; that what we desire may not necessarily be desirable; and the intensity and sincerity of prayer may be incommensurate for producing the desired effect. It will be foolish on our part to expect to be able to buy a big diamond by paying few peanuts. Similarly if we expect prayer to be effective the sincerity and intensity must be commensurate with the gain we are seeking.

The belief that God exists and has a role in our happiness is firmly etched on the collective consciousness of human beings. So long as we have to face death, so long as we feel helpless sometime or other during our lifetime there will be a need of a personal, powerful, kind, and merciful God. Because of our helplessness we cannot but seek help and we can only confidently seek help from a source which cannot fail us. That unfailing source we have named God. When we are invoking God's help we are tapping into our own higher nature by autosuggestion. Even the idea that someone powerful is looking after us provides us strength and confidence to face difficult situations. When we prepare ourselves to face difficult situations with confidence there is greater chance of success. We need that extra help to solve or cope up with our problems. However that extra help may not be necessary for everyone but those who do need it should make use of it. Seeking help from God is neither a mistake nor a superstition.

20

Handling of Our Internal Enemies

Anger, greed, delusion, vanity, and jealousy are our internal enemies lurking in our mind ready to pounce and mar our happiness. These internal enemies of ours are the progeny of desire. All our actions are prompted by desires. Anger is the result of an unfulfilled desire directed at the cause obstructing the fulfillment of a desire. Under the influence of anger one loses power of discrimination. With loss of discrimination the sense of what is right and what is wrong is lost and one is at risk at pursuing a wrong path. If a desire gets fulfilled one may forget that many factors are responsible for the success of one's action and claim the credit exclusively to oneself leading to arrogance. When we are in competition with others for fulfillment of a desire, success of others may give rise to jealousy in us or if we succeed we may be the victim of others' jealousy.

Since desire is the mother of all our internal enemies logically they can be got rid of by giving up desires. However, giving up of all desires is neither easy nor desirable. We have been endowed with power to know, power to do, and power to desire. Any power could be used for noble or ignoble purposes. We have to judiciously use these powers. There is nothing in nature which is intrinsically good or is intrinsically bad. Good and bad is only from our perspective. For example sugar is neither good nor bad. Too high or too low a level of sugar in our blood can prove lethal, but sugar within physiologic limits in our blood is most beneficial and is necessary for our well being. In this respect desire is similar to sugar. Desire within certain limits is most beneficial but outside of those limits is very harmful.

The first requisite is that the desire be in alignment with cosmic order (*dharma*). A desire is to be considered in alignment with cosmic order when it is inclusive. A desire which takes into account the welfare of the humanity as a whole will be in alignment with the cosmic order and not the one governed by selfishness. To earn money by legitimate means to feed One's family is in accordance with cosmic order whereas getting money by robbing a bank is not.

The second requisite is that even the desires which are in accordance with cosmic order should be pursued in moderation. We have to perform many different roles simultaneously such as parents, children, spouses etc. Unless moderation is practiced it will be difficult to give for all the roles the needed attention without causing some harm.

A picture is said to be worth thousand words. Importance of moderation is illustrated by the following episode. A physician was earning his living in a legitimate way. He wanted to be a good provider for his family. He provided them with a nice house, bought all amenities money could buy. In the process he ended up spending long hours in his profession and little time was left for his family. One day he entered his home to find it empty. On the dining table was the photograph of the expensive car he had recently bought for the family with the caption saying, "Nice car, but nowhere to go." His unhappy family had deserted him making him unhappy.

The third thing we have to remember about desire is that whenever we use a product some undesirable byproducts are generated and these byproducts must be effectively handled to prevent them from harming us. One example is the green gas effect produced by the use of fossil fuel. Regardless of fulfillment or nonfulfillment of our desires certain toxic byproducts may be generated not only in ourselves but also in others. These undesirable byproducts include anger, greed, vanity, narrow mindedness, and jealousy. Our success can make someone angry and jealous and their behavior could hurt us. When we succeed we may become vain, greedy and become narrow minded with concern for 'me' and' mine' and hurt others and ourselves. One effective method for neutralizing the effects of the toxic byproducts is by divinizing the world. This aspect will be dealt a little later in this chapter.

Anger

An action is a deliberate undertaking whereas a reaction is impulsive. In an action we will be in control whereas in a reaction we will be controlled. Anger is a reaction. Anger does not wait for our invitation to come. It happens. Therefore the advise 'do not become angry' is not of much help. What needs to be mastered is anger management. Anger management is very similar in many respects to disease management.

Every disease has a cause. The cause for anger is obstructed desire. Every disease causes some damage. The damage caused by anger includes physical or verbal pain to the victim of the anger. Anger can lead to irreparable damage to relationships cultivated over many years. The punishment inflicted under the influence of anger may be disproportionate and unfair for real or perceived offences of others paving the way for suffering from guilt feelings for the rest of one's life.

Treatment of any disease can be divided into two categories, namely, prophylactic and therapeutic. Prophylactic treatment includes improving general health by adopting health promoting habits and the use of vaccines to immunize against specific diseases.

What causes anger is not a given action but what we bring into that action based on our own biases and previous experiences. There will be trigger points in us when pressed gives rise to anger. It will be helpful to recognize these points. For example if one is prone to anger whenever a less than flattering remark concerning one's favorite sports team is made, then that is the trigger point for that person. If one were to find that there is risk that one's trigger point is about be pressed in a particular surrounding then one can leave that place and avoid the risk of becoming angry.

If one is not able to avoid the situation causing anger then other measures need to be put into practice which is comparable to treating a disease. One can maintain silence exercising vocal control with the realization that once a word escapes from our lips they can never be taken back. Any damage done by our words will be irreversible. So a cooling off period will be of immense help in avoiding saying or doing something which leads to pain and guilt feelings. One should decide to postpone taking any action only after a period of cooling. Even a few minutes of cooling will help. A helpful measure is the time honored advise to count to ten before taking any action while angry. Another helpful aid is to write down one's resentment and frustration on a paper and then destroying it. It is a harmless means for venting anger and regain composure.

Greed

The attitude of not sharing with others our possessions and wanting to accumulate more is greed. A greedy mind has the knack of breeding new demands in quick succession. Greed produces a sense of dissatisfaction which constantly poisons happiness. To overcome greed we have to understand that we do not possess anything and everything is temporarily given to us for our use. After using the item it has to be returned and not hoarded. If we do not part with it willingly it will be taken away forcibly causing pain and unhappiness. Happiness consists in giving back voluntarily. To overcome greed we have to practice charity which is in conformity with the cosmic plan of receiving and giving. Charity also helps in social redistribution of wealth and avoids social conflicts.

Delusion

We are under the false impression that our happiness depends on what we have. What we have may be lost or lose its value. But what we are could never be lost. Therefore our happiness depends not on what we have but on what we are. We should work on making ourselves better human beings much more than on accumulating things around us.

Vanity

This refers to the attitude that one is better than all others due to some success in one's actions. Vanity is a sign of immaturity of not realizing that for any success there are many contributing factors. And when a vain person meets someone with superior attributes the blow to the ego will result in extreme pain leading to jealousy. It is worth remembering that time is a universal devour of places, people and fame. The sonnet, Ozymandias, is worth contemplating concerning the fate of vain people.

Ozymandias

IN Egypt's sandy silence, all alone,

Stands a gigantic Leg, which far off throws

The only shadow that the Desert knows:—

"I am great OZYMANDIAS," saith the stone,

"The King of Kings; this mighty City shows

"The wonders of my hand."— The City's gone,—

Nought but the Leg remaining to disclose

The site of this forgotten Babylon.

We wonder,—and some Hunter may express

Wonder like ours, when thro' the wilderness

Where London stood, holding the Wolf in chace,

He meets some fragment huge, and stops to guess

What powerful but unrecorded race

Once dwelt in that annihilated place.

Horace Smith (1779-1849)

Jealousy

This results from comparison. Differences are inherent in nature and have to be accepted as a fact of life. Any comparison will lead to either superiority or inferiority complex. Jealousy leads to unhealthy competition begetting negative emotions of anger, deceit, and ill feelings etc. Cooperation is preferable to competition.

There are disease causing bacteria all around us. It is not possible to eliminate all of them to ensure disease free existence. However, we can decrease the risk of infection by improving our immune system by following healthy habits. Similarly divinizing the world helps us to cope up with our internal enemies. What the expression 'divinizing the world' means is accepting that there is an intelligence principle guiding this world. Acceptance of an intelligence principle, popularly referred to as God, guiding the world has an important corollary and many advantages.

The corollary is that the situations we find ourselves are not random but planned and we are part of the plan. There is an order governing this creation. In this order each one of us is uniquely created endowed with special qualities for fulfilling the plan and purpose of the creation. What we have received for fulfilling the plan and purpose of creation is different, but what we are is the same namely an instrument in the hands of God. We are endowed with free will to determine our extent of participation in the plan and purpose of the creation.

One advantage of considering ourselves as an instrument of God is equanimity of mind we will gain in our success and failures. Both our success and failure does serve an important purpose in the large scheme of things and we can derive satisfaction that we have done our part. Our attitude will be one of "Not my but thy will shall be done." With such an attitude there is no reason for getting puffed up with pride with success or depressed with failure. This attitude is conducive for development of humility. Ignorance of this fact leads to vanity.

Another advantage is freedom from jealousy. Jealousy is a product of comparison leading to a sense of victimization. The thought that everything belongs to God and is given to individuals based on their capacity for purposes of fulfilling the grand plan is an antidote for jealousy. We will be appreciating everyone's success as that of our own near and dear ones. There will be no room for jealousy in the knowledge that we have our talents just as others have theirs. Every talent is for serving the plan and purpose of the creation. Each is great in his own sphere and there is no reason for jealousy.

The realization that no success is possible without the contribution and cooperation of multiple factors governing the creation is a powerful antidote to the problem of vanity. If we were to understand that an obstructed desire is part of the cosmic order then we will be able to cope up without anger and its undesirable consequences. Viewing the actions of other people as part of the larger picture will free us from disappointment and becoming judgmental. Realization that everything is given to us for our temporary use and we did not bring anything into this world is an antidote for greed and makes practice of charity easier. The awareness that there is an order and that there is a penalty to be paid for infringement of the order is a powerful motive to lead a virtuous life with its associated benefits including happiness.

Realization that the will of God will never take us to where the grace of God will not protect us is a wonderful stress reliever. Imagine a railroad car with human qualities but ignorant of the engine pulling the whole train.

That ignorant car thinks that it is responsible for pulling the car behind it and pushing the car in front of it. How can such a car be relaxed? However the moment the car realizes that it is the engine that is pulling the whole train and it has to just go along with other cars, the relaxation it feels will be instantaneous. Similarly when we realize that there is a propelling force directing the creation and we have to just go along with it will greatly reduce our stress and allows us to live in the present with its consequent advantages.

What Is Living in the Present?

As human beings, we have to play different roles such as children, parents, spouse, employer, employee etc. For a harmonious living our behavior should be in accordance with the role we are called upon to play. As our roles change, the thoughts in our mind should change appropriate for the role. Fortunately mind has the capacity to change as the role changes. When the mind is changing in accordance with the role to be played, the mind will be available to us and we will be living in the present. Unless the mind changes with the role to be played, awkward and even dangerous situations could arise. For instance a man because of an argument with his wife becomes angry. At that time he is enacting the role of an angry husband. In his anger he leaves the house and starts driving his car to work. When he is driving the car he is a driver. Though physically he is a driver mentally he still remains an angry husband. There is disassociation between body and mind. Mind is not available to him for the task at hand. Because of disconnection between the role he is playing and the thoughts he is harboring, that person is not living in the present. Because of this disconnection a serious accident can happen. We are living in the present when body and mind are together. When there is a disassociation between body and mind we are not living in the present.

Why Is It Important to be Living in the Present?

When we are living in the present our life will be efficient and harmonious. While living in the present our actions will be appropriate for the role we will be playing. There will be harmony between the role and its action. Harmony is another word for happiness, which is desired by one and all.

The impediments for living in the present include:

1. Guilt and hurt feelings of the past.
2. Anxiety about the future.
3. Mechanical aimless thinking.

Guilt and Hurt Feelings of the Past

We are born as babes; pass our childhood under the control of people who are bigger and stronger having enormous influence on us. During our interactions with these people there will be real or perceived instances of unfair treatment. Since at that stage of our life we cannot retaliate against the real or perceived injustice the resentment gets suppressed in our subconscious. Because of such experiences we do not see the world as it is, but through our colored glasses of impressions created by our own experiences. Our judgments based on our biases govern our behavior. Even when we have grown up as adults the impressions left behind by those experiences might not have resolved. They may remain in our psyche and are triggered by people or events. When triggered the adult regresses to childhood and the behavior will be that of a child rather than that of a mature adult. This phenomenon is called transference and is the basis for exaggerated response we see in individuals for a seemingly trivial event. Because of our biases we become hostage to our past. Instead of responding freshly to situations as they are encountered we will be responding inappropriately predisposing ourselves to sadness, disappointment, resentment, jealousy, unhappiness and other undesirable effects. When we feel that we are victims of ill treatment we suffer from feelings of hurt. When we have failed to live our lives according to our value systems, we suffer from guilt feelings. These hurt and guilt feelings generate in us anger, jealousy, hatred, resentment etc.

Anxiety of the Future

Mind becomes unavailable to us because of its tendency to worry about the future. The worry is due to the uncertainty about the future. And the uncertainty stems from our limited knowledge and ability to control and alter the future events.

Mechanical Aimless Thinking (Chattering of Mind)

Mind is nothing but a series of thoughts. It wanders from thought to thought in a random fashion accomplishing nothing. Unless we are vigilant, mind starts to brood over the past which cannot be changed or fantasizes about the future which is uncertain. Not living in the present is inefficient living squandering opportunities for making ourselves better and happy.

Clues for Living in the Present

To live in the present means responding to people and situations with a fresh alert mind free from the hurt and guilt feelings of the past and anxieties about the future. Living in the present is harmonious living. Harmonious living is living happily. We are happy when we are acceptable to ourselves. We are acceptable to ourselves when we have lived a life of our true nature. Our true nature is to be kind. That is the reason why we feel happy when someone tells us that we are kind. When someone tells the contrary we become unhappy. Anger, jealousy, hatred etc. are alien to our true nature. When swayed by such undesirable characteristics we become unacceptable to ourselves and unhappy. We cannot expect the world to change to meet our demands. It has its own rhythm. The only alternative is to change ourselves. To become acceptable to ourselves we have to lead a life free from negative emotions and cultivate positive emotions.

An important technique for getting rid of a negative emotion and for developing a positive emotion is to deliberately replace negative emotion by its positive counterpart (*pratipakshabhava*). For example hatred must be replaced by feelings of love. The change must be sincerely expressed. Suppose we have hatred towards someone or someone hates us. If we keep on showing gestures of good will sooner or later hatred will disappear making way for the emotion of affection and love. While Mahatma Gandhi was working for racial equality in South Africa his adversary was General Smuts. Gandhi was imprisoned by General Smuts. Gandhi while he was imprisoned made a pair of sandals for General Smut and sent it to him. Later while he was writing an essay on the occasion to commemorate Gandhi's 70th birthday, General Smut wrote: "I have worn these sandals for many a summer, even though I feel that I am not worthy to stand in the shoes of so great a man." Gandhi had successfully converted his adversary into an admirer by nurturing the positive emotion of love instead of hatred towards General Smuts who was responsible for Gandhi's imprisonment. By this incidence Gandhi has demonstrated to us that one can disagree without being disagreeable. It is not easy to overcome negative emotions and furthermore even our sincere attempts to mend the situation may be viewed with skepticism and suspicion. However the attempt should be pursued with diligence with an alert mind with confidence. With practice a life dominated by positive emotions becomes spontaneous resulting in harmonious happy living.

Part 3

yad yad Acharti Sresthah tat tat eva itara janah
(Common folks imitate the action of virtuous people.)

It is important to have good role models. They can have profound influence in shaping our life. Mahatma Gandhi's life of service and truthfulness was shaped by the mythological figures of Sravana and Harischandra respectively. Study of the life history of great men and women has the added advantage of making abstract principles concrete.

21

Actions Speak Louder Than Words

An adolescent boy, for health reasons, was advised by his physician to refrain from eating salt. Since without salt food tastes insipid and the boy found it difficult to refrain from salt. He was not following the instructions of the physician as he should. His parents were concerned that his lack of adherence to the physician's recommendation would make his condition worse. So they tried to persuade him from eating salt by telling him to follow physician's advice. Their efforts proved to be of no avail.

The father of the boy was a friend of Mahatma Gandhi and the boy had great respect for the Mahatma. The father thought that if Mahatma Gandhi were to ask the boy to refrain from salt the boy would do so. Then he explained the situation to Gandhi and requested him to tell the boy to refrain from salt. Gandhi agreed. Few days passed by but Gandhi had not told the boy to refrain from salt. The father reminded Gandhi of his request and could not understand why Gandhi was taking so much of time to do the simple task of telling the boy to refrain from salt. Whenever he was reminded, Gandhi assured the father that he will tell the boy. A month had passed and Gandhi had not yet told the boy to refrain from salt. The father of the boy was frustrated. At the end of one month Gandhi sent for the boy. When the boy came Gandhi told him to refrain from eating salt. The boy in an angry tone said, "Do you know how difficult it is to refrain from eating salt? It is easy for you to say to me to refrain from eating salt." Gandhi replied, "Yes I do know. Your father asked me to tell you to refrain from eating salt about a month ago. I have during the past month refrained from eating salt. If I can do it you too can do it." The boy was moved knowing that for his sake Gandhi had refrained from eating salt which his own parents had not done. He gave up eating salt.

The incidence illustrates the superiority of action over words in shaping our lives. We may not be lucky enough to come in contact with people of the caliber of Gandhi for our benefit. However we can benefit from studying the life history of great people to shape our lives. Their actions and achievements will inspire and serve us to exploit our full potential for leading a happier life.

22

Vishwamitra

In the days of yore there lived a king by name Kaushika. Once he was touring his country with his retinue. During his tour he came across the abode (*Ashram*) of the great sage Vasista. The *Ashram* was lovely and peaceful. According to the custom of those days no king would pass an *Ashram* without paying his homage to the sage of the *Ashram*. In accordance with the custom of the day Kaushika visited Vasista in his *Ashram*. Kaushika was warmly welcomed by Vasista. After they had enquired about each other's welfare and discussed topics of mutual interest, Kaushika sought permission of the sage to leave. However Vasista insisted that the king and his retinue should not leave without accepting his hospitality. Kaushika was eager to leave not wanting to trouble the ascetic sage of having to feed his large retinue but relented on Vasista's insistence.

Vasista was in possession of a divine cow called Surabhi. The cow had the magical power of fulfilling any wish. The cow, given to Vasista by Gods, was providing him materials needed for performing rituals for the welfare of humanity. Vasista asked the cow to produce food and drinks for feeding the retinue of the king. In no time with her divine power Surabhi produced drinks and dishes of all kinds to the delight of every palate. The king and his retinue had never tasted such delicious sumptuous dishes and they were very pleased. After seeing the power of Surabhi Kaushika became greedy and wanted to possess the cow. He approached Vasista and said, "Oh great sage, you are a man of renunciation. As an ascetic you are required to renounce all material possessions. I, as a king, am responsible to feed a large number of people. If I have Surabhi it will benefit more people. So please give Surabhi to me. I will give you one thousand cows in exchange."

Vasista replied, "Surabhi is given to me by Gods to provide me with materials needed for the rituals I do for the welfare of humanity. Even if I want to give her I cannot. She will not part from me."

Kaushika persisted for some time trying to convince Vasista to part with Surabhi but did not succeed. He became angry and ordered his soldiers to cease the cow by force. Surabhi was grief stricken at the thought of being separated from Vasista. She freed herself from the hold of soldiers and came running to Vasista. With tears in her eyes she said, "Oh father why are you sending me away. What mistake have I committed?" Vasista consoled her by saying that she had not committed any mistake and Kaushika is taking her by force. Then Surabhi sought permission from Vasista to create an army for self protection and the permission was granted. The army created by Surabhi wiped out Kaushika's army. Kaushika was crestfallen. But his desire to possess Surabhi only got stronger.

He did penance to please Gods and obtained from them weapons to avenge his defeat. Armed with new and powerful weapons he, without notice, mounted an assault on Vasista's *Ashram*. Vasista, the great sage, used his spiritual power to neutralize all of Kaushika's weapons. Kaushika had the bitter taste of defeat for the second time. However he realized the superiority of spiritual power over physical power and decided to gain spiritual power similar to that of Vasista. He resorted to penance again. Pleased with his penance creator Brahma granted him the title of raja rishi which is far inferior to Vasista's status of Brahma rishi.

Kaushika was not satisfied with what he had gained. He continued his penance. While he was thus engaged a king named Trishanku approached him and sought his help. Trishanku had the strange desire of going to heaven with his mortal body. Earlier he had approached Vasista to help him realize his desire. Vasista had declined to help since Trishanku's desire was not in conformity with the order of creation. Trishanku then approached Vasista's sons to help him ascend to heaven in his mortal body. They too had declined since one cannot enter heaven with a mortal body. Trishanku narrated his sad story to Kaushika who agreed to help him. Kaushika thought this was an opportunity for him to show to the world that he could do what Vasista could not and establish his superiority. Kaushika arranged and officiated over a special sacrificial ritual to send Trishanku to heaven. However the Gods did not approve of Kaushika's action and did not come to take Trishanku to heaven as expected by Kaushika. Angered by the lack of response on the part of Gods in taking Trishanku to heaven, using his accumulated spiritual power he made Trishanku to ascend towards heaven like a missile. However when Trishanku reached the gates of heaven he was forcibly driven away by the Gods and he started to fall towards the earth. Further enraged by the act of Gods Kaushika made the falling Trishanku stay in mid air and started building a new heaven for Trishanku. Then the Gods and Kaushika reached a compromise. The terms of compromise were that Kaushika would stop expanding the already built new heaven and the Gods would leave Trishanku undisturbed in his own heaven. At the end of this episode Kaushika had used up all his spiritual powers and his spiritual treasury had become empty. He had to start all over again.

Undaunted Kaushika began his penance once again. He was accumulating spiritual powers again. Gods wanted to test his will power to resist temptations. They sent Menaka, the beautiful celestial nymph, for this purpose. She came to where Kaushika was engaged in penance and started moving about in his vicinity. Kaushika was enchanted by her good looks and sweet voice. He forgot his penance and started to live with her enjoying pleasures of the flesh. Ten years went by and a baby girl was born to them. By now he was spiritually bankrupt for the second time. Then Kaushika realized the mistake he had made. He left Menaka and started penance all over again.

He was making progress with his penance. Gods again wanted to test him. This time they sent Rambha another celestial nymph to test his power of self control. When he saw Rambha he remembered what had happened to him with Menaka. He realized that this was a plot of Gods to distract from his goal. He became angry and cursed Rambha to become a stone. Along with losing his temper he also lost the accumulated spiritual strength. Not willing to give up he restarted his penance again. After having done penance for a long time he became hungry and cooked some food to eat. Just before he was about to eat a pious man came begging for food. Although hungry Kaushika gave the food he had cooked to that pious man without resentment or regret maintaining silence. The pious man was none other than Indra, the chief of Gods. Pleased with the restraint Kaushika had developed Gods pronounced him to be fit to become a Brahma rishi, the status he had strived for so long. However they put a condition for granting that status. The condition was that Vasista had to approve that Kaushika had become eligible to gain the status of Brahma rishi. This was the last and difficult hurdle Kaushika had to face. It was not easy for him to approach Vasista, his adversary of the past, and seek his approval. Because of his vanity it was very difficult for Kaushika to approach Vasista for gaining his approval. He feared that Vasista, whom he had wronged in the past may not grant his approval. But he had no other choice. With trepidation he proceeded towards Vasista's *Ashram* and reached there by dusk. Still hesitant to approach Vasista, he paused for sometime behind a bush in the *Ashram*. Then he overheard the conversation between Vasista and his wife who passed by the bush.

Vasista's wife said, "I heard that Gods are prepared to grant the status of Brahma rishi to Kaushika if he were to get your approval. Would you give your approval if he approached you despite everything that has happened between you two?"

Vasista replied, "Certainly I will give my approval. You know that people change. To judge the present Kaushika, who has accomplished so much now, based on his past action is unfair. I never harbored any enmity towards him. I just disproved of his unrighteous actions. We should live in the present and not in the past. If he approaches me I will certainly approve of his gaining the status of a Brahma rishi, a status he richly deserves based on his accomplishments."

Kaushika was moved by the large heart of Vasista and overcame his vanity. He learnt the importance of living in the present and not be burdened by the past actions. Kaushika approached Vasista who welcomed him warmly and pronounced Kaushika to be a Brahma rishi. Kaushika was happy and then did many good deeds for humanity. Because of the good deeds he did he came to be known as Vishwamitra which means friend of the universe.

The purpose of mythological stories is to make abstract principles concrete. This mythological story of Kaushika makes many abstract principles concrete for us. Kaushika was a happy king until he had met Vasista in his *Ashram.* When he came to know of the powers of Surabhi he wanted to possess her. We can only desire a thing which we do know exists. Desire to posses arises when there is contact between sense objects and sense organs. Kaushika had no desire to possess Surabhi when he did not know of her existence. Once the desire to possess her arose in his mind he could not rest in peace. When his desire to possess Surabhi was not fulfilled he became angry. Anger is nothing but obstructed desire. Desire prompts us to action. Kaushika tried to take her forcibly but failed. We should have discrimination to accept that not all our desires get fulfilled; nor is it necessary to fulfill all our desires; and it is better to abandon desires that are inimical to harmonious existence. To take something from someone forcibly is a sign of lack of discrimination. Under the influence of anger Kaushika had lost the power of discrimination as to what is right and what is wrong. Kaushika did penance to gain weapons to subdue Vasista. He attacked Vasista for the second time. Our means for gaining an end must be proper. Kaushika relied on physical power. He had not realized that spiritual power is more potent than physical power. He learnt that bitter lesson when he found out that his physical power was not potent to subdue Vasista. Then he made the wise decision to gain spiritual power. But wishing does not produce the desired result. For success sustained effort is needed. The episodes concerning Trishanku, Menaka, and Rambha illustrate the consequences of lapses in our effort. Happiness requires a prepared mind.

We do not automatically get what we desire. We have to become deserving of our desires. We have to persist with our efforts as Kaushika did. His act of giving up food for the hungry person is symbolic of his getting over likes and dislikes and having developed equanimity of mind —a prerequisite for happiness. His final act of seeking acceptance from Vasista is symbolic of overcoming our ego which creates a division between us and the rest of the creation. The more we identify of our oneness with the creation which is an organic whole the greater will be our happiness. When we have reached that stage we will not be working for happiness but out of happiness as Vishwamitra did.

23

Mother Teresa
(1910 -1997)

Agnes Gonxha Bojaxhiu, who later became famous all over the world as Mother Teresa for her humanitarian work, was born to an Albanian catholic parents on August 26th 1910. When she was about 8 years old her father unexpectedly passed away. Her mother sustained the family by selling textiles and handmade embroideries. The family was deeply religious and was tightly knit. By the age of 12 years she had developed a strong urge to become a nun. However the decision to become a nun was not easy as it required her to relinquish hopes of marriage and raising her own family. Furthermore, the possibility of being separated from her mother made the decision all the more difficult. She thought about the idea of becoming a nun for the next five years. At age 17 she made the difficult decision of becoming a nun. She wanted to work as a missionary in India; a decision influenced by her becoming acquainted with the missionary work done by Irish nuns in India. When she was 18 she left for Ireland to join Loreto Order of nuns saying good bye to her family. She never saw them again. She arrived in India on January 6th, 1929. She took the vows of Loreto nuns in 1931. Then she began teaching history and geography at Entally convent in Calcutta (now renamed Kolkata). In 1937 she took final vows and officially became "Mother Teresa." After taking her final vows she became the principal of Saint Mary's convent. She was restricted to live within the confines of the convent as was the case when she was teaching in Entally convent earlier.

For nine years she worked as the principal at Saint Mary's convent. Once while she was travelling by train to Darjeeling she felt an inner urge to leave the convent and to help the poor living amidst them. She then petitioned her superiors for permission to leave the convent to begin her work among the poor. However, her superiors thought that it was a dangerous proposition for a woman, that too a single woman, to work in the slums of Calcutta. After two years of patient correspondence she obtained permission to leave the convent for a period of one year for helping the poor.

Prior to commencing her work in the slums of Calcutta she wanted to gain some medical experience. So she went to Patna and spent several weeks with the Medical Mission Sisters to gain basic medical knowledge. At the age 38 years Mother Teresa ventured out into the slums in 1948. While walking around the slum she found few small children and began teaching them despite the handicap of not having a class room, chalk board, paper, pencil, and other amenities. She picked up a stick and began drawing letters on the ground covered with dust. She later found a small hut for her class room. She visited families and offered medical help within her ability. People came to know the service she was rendering and began making donations for her cause. By the end of her provisionary year few others had joined her in her work and she petitioned to form her own order of nuns by name Missionaries of Charity. Her request was granted. Missionaries of Charity came into existence on Oct 7th 1950.

She opened a home for the dying in 1952 and named it Nirmal Hriday. Each day the nuns would walk the streets of Calcutta and bring the dying destitute to the home. They would wash them, feed them, and place them on a cot. Destitute people were given an opportunity to die with dignity observing rituals of their faith.

Mother Teresa expanded the scope of her service by opening her first children home in 1955 to care for orphaned children. Children were cared for physically, emotionally, and were taught skills to earn a living in addition to attempts at finding suitable homes for their adoption. Moved by the plight of lepers she established a number of mobile leper clinics for the purpose of delivering medicine and bandages to lepers near their homes. A leper colony named Shanti Nagar was established for lepers to live and work in 1960.

Approximately ten years after the establishment of Missionaries of Charity permission was granted for establishing centers outside Calcutta but within India. Soon centers were established in several major cities of India. Five years later permission was granted to establish centers outside India as well. By the time of Mother Teresa's demise (September 5th, 1997) the order of Missionaries of Charity had 4000 nuns working from 610 centers in 123 countries. She was awarded Nobel Peace Prize in 1979 for her humanitarian work. Though she had accomplished a lot, Mother Teresa never took personal credit for her work. **She believed that it was God working through her; she being only a tool.**

Mother Teresa's life proves certain important facts. One is that happiness depends not what we have but what we are. She had little possessions but was happy rendering care to the destitute. Her life depicts the close relationship needed for success of any goal and the life style. Her life is an example that the effects produced by our efforts are not all immediate but may be delayed. Without being discouraged we should persist with our efforts. Her life further illustrates that the creation is an organic whole and any good we do selflessly cannot but enrich our own lives in addition to that of others. Her life illustrates the strength one gains from belief in God for accomplishing one's cherished goals and remain happy.

24

Sri. Ramakrishna Paramahamsa (1836 -1886)

In a remote village called Kamarpukuron, located in India, on Feb 18th 1836 a boy was born to a poor, pious couple who named him Gadhadhara who is now well known as Sri. Ramakrishna Paramahamsa. As a boy he was the darling of the whole village. He was the center of attention of both boys and girls of his age. He had good memory. He sang devotional songs with a sweet voice. He was artistic in nature and took interest in clay modeling and enacting drama. He showed little interest in formal education. Once when he was rebuked by his elder brother for neglecting secular studies he had said that he did not care for mere bread winning education. **He wanted that education which would illumine his heart and give spiritual satisfaction; an education which will lift him above all wants.** He had little formal education. When he was 17 years of age, Sri. Ramakrishna was taken to Calcutta by his elder brother to be his assistant in a Sanskrit school he was managing. But Sri. Ramakrishna liked to engage himself in the worship of God in the family temple. When three years had passed after his coming to Calcutta, a rich lady completed building a temple for Goddess Kali in

Dakheneswar on the outskirts of Calcutta. Sri. Ramakrishna became the priest in that temple. His devotion to the Goddess was exceptional. During his free time from the duties of the temple, especially at night, he retired to a solitary spot to meditate. As time passed he behaved with the idol of the Goddess as if it was a living person forgetful of time and surroundings. He was seized with the idea that if God is real God must be realized as the substantive of all existence. If God is intelligent and responsive, God must respond to the yearnings of the prayerful devotees. During one of his spiritual practices he had the vision of God as the totality and he described his experience as having experienced intense bliss never experienced before. **During that experience all things around him had disappeared and he saw only boundless infinite consciousness all around.**

During the time of his intense spiritual exercises he wept frequently unable to bear separation from God he was worshiping. His behavior made others think that he was becoming insane. It is natural for people to see insanity in anyone whose behavior is not in conformity with that of their own be it abnormal or supernormal. Because of concern for his mental health he was sent to his village to rest and recuperate. While in the village he was noted to be his old loving self. His relatives thought that if Sri. Ramakrishna got married, the burden of domestic responsibilities will make him lead a life similar to theirs. They had difficulty finding a bride for him because of the rumor that he was mentally unstable. Sri. Ramakrishna, who had gained supernatural powers by his austerities including the power to see the future, solved the problem by telling them that his bride is Sharada Devi, (whom he had not seen earlier) the daughter of Ramachandra upadhyaya of Jayarambati. Marriage of Sri. Ramakrishna with Sharada Devi was celebrated.

After a lapse of two years Sri. Ramakrishna returned to Dakheneswar to resume his duties as the priest. Divine madness which had abated during his absence from Dakheneswar returned with redoubled vehemence. At about this time the arrival of Bhairavi Brahmini, a sanyasini, was of great importance in Sri. Ramakrishna's life. With her knowledge of scriptures and her spiritual eminence she convinced others that Sri. Ramkrishna's mental status was not insanity but divine intoxication.

Under the guidance of Brahmini and others Sri. Ramkrishna was initiated to the spiritual discipline and practice of different religions including Christianity and Islam. He followed them with insatiable gusto and mastered them in a relatively short period of time. Based on the insight he gained from such practices he declared that different religions are different paths to the realization of the same God. His message is that we should consider followers of other religions as fellow pilgrims to the same destination through different roads. If his words had been heeded the world would have been a much safer and happier place for all humanity.

The relationship between Sri. Ramakrishna and his wife Sharada Devi was unique. Sri. Ramakrishna had once asked her on arrival to Dakheneswar, "Do you want to drag me to worldly life?" She had replied, "Why should I do that?" I have come to serve you and to be of help to you in your spiritual life." She in turn had asked him, "How do you look upon me?" His reply was, "The Mother who is worshiped in the temple, the Mother who gave birth to this body, and you who are attending on me are alike to me." Their questions and answers was a literal expression of their respective attitude and outlook on their lives. It was not a casual conversation to suit the occasion of the moment.

Sri. Ramakrishna after completing his spiritual practices had an urge to share his realization with others for the benefit of humanity. Devotees began coming to him for spiritual guidance. He had prevision of several of his disciples who were to come seeking his guidance. He had many devotees and disciples. Outstanding among them was his monastic disciples who like the branches of a mighty tree grew to spread his spiritual genius. Of his sixteen monastic disciples the most well known is Swami Vivekananda who became the star of the first parliament of religions held in Chicago and was a force in reviving spirituality in the world. Sri. Ramakrishna's method of teaching was unique and was done through informal conversations using familiar everyday experiences to explain difficult spiritual truths. He did not resort to formal lectures, discourses or scriptural expositions. His teaching had the force of his first hand experience.

He was ever a center of joy and inspiration. He never forced his views on anyone. He had the strange capacity to cater to the spiritual needs of people of diverse temperaments and intellectual development. In spite of his ecstasies and divine intoxication he paid minute attention to details of life. He was very particular about personal cleanliness and orderliness of things kept in his room.

Sri. Ramakrishna developed cancer of the throat and succumbed to that disease on 16th August 1886. During his terminal illness he was advised to rest his voice. But he did not stop singing devotional songs, talking to devotees, and teaching his disciples. He remained active until the very end. His disciples requested him to pray to Goddess Mother for his recovery. He told them that such a prayer could not come from his lips as he had surrendered his body and mind to the Mother long ago. However when Naren (later Swami Vivekananda) kept on insisting Sri Ramakrishna relented a little. He prayed to Mother to enable him to consume some food to maintain strength to teach others. He communicated to his disciples what the Mother had said in response to his prayers. Her saying was, "Are you not taking food through all these mouths. Why do you think of taking food through this one mouth?" A fitting reply for a man established in oneness with the creation—an organic whole.

For the majority of us happiness consists in satisfying our instinctive desires as fully and as successfully to the maximum extent possible. However happiness derived from satisfying such desires is undependable and is the cause of much misery and suffering for ourselves and others. Sri. Ramakrishna, lacking formal education, lacking riches, and coming from a remote village has shown us the existence of a higher state of happiness available to us at the level of our spiritual personality. He exemplifies that the higher state of happiness becomes available by identifying ourselves with that entity which provides coherence to all that exists and is called God in religion. Mere intellectual understanding of the entity is not sufficient. The information gained by understanding should result in transformation in our living. The transformation requires us to conduct ourselves not as separate entities but as an integral part of the existence which is an organic whole. Sri. Ramakrishna achieved the transformation with intense effort. Although no one is barred from achieving what he achieved, it may not be possible for majority of us because of lack of preparation. What Sri. Ramakrishna achieved and demonstrated to us must be kept in mind as our potential to be realized and begin our journey towards that goal.

25

Salient Points

1. Desire for happiness is universal and legitimate.

2. We seek happiness because it is our true nature. What is natural is never a burden.

3. Unhappiness is an intruder of happiness just as disease is that of health and sound is that of silence.

4. To be happy what is needed is the elimination of the intruder—unhappiness. To gain silence we do not need to do anything other than stop making noise. When we stop making noise silence automatically ensues.

5. Unhappiness is the penalty we are paying for transgressing the law that the whole of the creation is one integrated, interrelated, organic whole. We are transgressing the law by feeling and acting as independent, separate, isolated entities.

6. To be happy we should stop violating the law.

7. We are violating the law because of our ignorance of the dynamics of happiness and the consequent mistakes we are committing. The mistakes we are committing include:

a. Searching for happiness in the wrong places: What we want is enduring happiness which is freedom from all our insecurities based on our perceived limitations. We search security in objects in the world outside of ourselves. The irony is that the objects we seek for our security are themselves ever changing, perishable, and impermanent. How can impermanent objects give us enduring happiness? Any number of impermanent objects put together cannot become permanent; they remain impermanent. We are searching for the permanent among the impermanent. Naturally we fail in our search, become disappointed and dissatisfied.

b. Not being clear in our thinking as to what happiness is: We feel happy when we gain an object of our desire. But the happiness so gained is transient. We remain seekers of happiness. The divide between the seeker and the sought continues. We remain in the process of becoming which implies dissatisfaction with our present status. We want to become more acceptable to ourselves. What we want to become lies in our uncertain future. And since we may not gain what we want to become, the result is anxiety, worry and unhappiness. By our constant focus at becoming more acceptable to ourselves, we miss out on the beauty of the present. This is a price we pay for our efforts at becoming rather than being rooted in our "being". The meaning of being rooted in our "being" is accepting ourselves as we are without being judgmental and then trying to improve ourselves.

c. Our misguided dependence on objects for happiness: Because of our misplaced reliance on objects of the world for our happiness we are conditioned to accumulate objects. The tendency to accumulate is encouraged and reinforced by the consumer culture we live in. Commercial enterprises through the medium of advertisements bombard us with the message that an increase in consumption/possessions increases our happiness. This assumption is fallacious. Presence or absence of material objects does not bring happiness or unhappiness. There are many instances of wealthy people being unhappy in spite of their possessions and even committing suicide in despair. Great saints, sages, and prophets renounced everything and without any possessions discovered happiness. Buddha, to mention one example, renounced his kingdom with all the luxuries associated with it for the sake of enduring happiness. Such great men and women enjoyed happiness because they touched within themselves the source of happiness. To become happy we should shift our attention from pursuit of goods to pursuit of goodness. Once again, I do not want to give the impression that to be happy one should renounce all material possessions. By themselves material possessions are not the problem. It is the craving for material possessions that causes unhappiness and stands between us and our happiness. It has been aptly said that it is not the person who has less, but the person who craves more is poor. Material possessions have a useful role in our lives. They are needed for our very survival. However we should make a distinction between our "needs" and "wants". Needs are those that are essential for our survival and growth. Wants are those things that are extra—that gratify our desires. To protect ourselves from the elements we need clothes. Clothing is a need. But the desire to wear designer clothes is a want. The balance between our needs and wants has to be discovered by each one of us and not by anyone else. It is a personal choice. Living with either too little or too much is a hindrance for a happier life. If our energy were to be totally expended in struggle for survival our capacity to think of higher things in life gets diminished or even may be lost completely. On the other hand too much attention for accumulating possessions will leave little time and energy to contemplate higher things in life—developing goodness within ourselves. The goods we posses may be lost by being stolen by thieves confiscated by government, destroyed by natural disasters and by the claim of our relatives for their share. They may lose value by market forces. But the goodness in us, such as kindness, compassion, empathy etc. which we should develop to be happy can never be stolen, confiscated nor can a share of it be claimed by others. This is the difference between the impermanent goods we accumulate and the permanent goodness we cultivate. For a person of discrimination the choice would be clearly evident.

8. The remedy: To be happy we have to be inconformity with the law that the whole of the creation in an integrated interrelated organic whole. To be in conformity of the law we have to bring about a cognitive change in our thinking and the thinking should lead to transformation in our lives. The change requires us to become more and more inclusive and less and less exclusive. We become inclusive when we develop divine qualities such as kindness, compassion, love etc. and giving up opposite qualities. Conformity to the law leads to happiness and resistance to unhappiness. We are free to either conform or resist. The choice is ours. **In summary to be happy or unhappy is our choice.**

sarve bhavantu sukhinah
sarve santu nirAmayah
sarve bhadraNI pashantu
mA dhukha bhagbhavet.

(May everyone be happy
May everyone be free from afflictions
May everyone experience auspiciousness
Let no one experience misery.)